MAXIMIZING YOUR SALES WITH SALESFORCE.COM®

Edward Kachinske | Stacy Roach

Carol Gilliland | Timothy Kachinske

Course Technology PTR

A part of Cengage Learning

COURSE TECHNOLOGY
CENGAGE Learning™

Australia, Brazil, Japan, Korea, Mexico, Singapore, Spain, United Kingdom, United States

COURSE TECHNOLOGY
CENGAGE Learning™

Maximizing Your Sales with Salesforce.com
Edward Kachinske, Stacy Roach,
Carol Gilliland, Timothy Kachinske

Publisher and General Manager, Course Technology PTR:
Stacy L. Hiquet

Associate Director of Marketing:
Sarah Panella

Manager of Editorial Services:
Heather Talbot

Marketing Manager:
Mark Hughes

Acquisitions Editor:
Mitzi Koontz

Project Editor:
Jenny Davidson

Technical Reviewers:
Brad Mattick and Steve Stroz

PTR Editorial Services Coordinator:
Erin Johnson

Interior Layout Tech:
Bill Hartman

Cover Designer:
Mike Tanamachi

Indexer:
Katherine Stimson

Proofreader:
Sara Gullion

For product information and technology assistance, contact us at
Cengage Learning Customer & Sales Support Center, 1-800-354-9706

For permission to use material from this text or product, submit all requests online at **cengage.com/permissions**
Further permissions questions can be emailed to
permissionrequest@cengage.com

Salesforce.com is a registered trademark of Salesforce.com. All other trademarks are the property of their respective owners.

Library of Congress Control Number: 2008902387

ISBN-13: 978-1-59863-562-1

ISBN-10: 1-59863-562-X

Course Technology
25 Thomson Place
Boston, MA 02210
USA

Cengage Learning is a leading provider of customized learning solutions with office locations around the globe, including Singapore, the United Kingdom, Australia, Mexico, Brazil, and Japan. Locate your local office at: **international.cengage.com/region**

Cengage Learning products are represented in Canada by Nelson Education, Ltd.

For your lifelong learning solutions, visit **courseptr.com**

Visit our corporate website at **cengage.com**

Printed in the United States of America
1 2 3 4 5 6 7 11 10 09 08

This book is dedicated to my mother, Judith Kachinske. She's one of the smartest people I know, and she has a big heart. Her moral compass is better than mine, and she's on a short list of people who will always tell me when I'm wrong. She's always been there for me, and for that I am more grateful than she probably even realizes.

—EK

This book is dedicated to Stacy and Max. Stacy has taught me so much about life, love, right, and wrong. I could not imagine my life without her. She is the salt for my meat. And Max has made my heart get bigger and my life more filled with joy. Thank you to both of you for what you have given me.

—CJG

This book is dedicated to my family. First, to Carol, who is the most amazing person I know, and I am the luckiest girl alive because she is in my life. For Max, who is such a wonderful young man; it is a privilege to watch you as you grow and mature. For my parents, Dick and LaVerne, for teaching me about hard work, ethics, family, and love. And for my two brothers, Matt and E.T., for never letting me get too big for my britches.

—SAR

Acknowledgments

This is my 23rd published title and fourth book with Course Technology PTR. It's been a true pleasure working with Stacy Hiquet, Mitzi Koontz, and the whole team. A big hug goes out to all of you. You really are the best in the business.

It's been great working with our project editor, Jenny Davidson. When Jenny reads this paragraph, it will mark the third time she has edited me thanking her for a job well done. Thanks…again. I hope we will work together on the next project.

Brad Mattick, who probably knows more about Salesforce than anyone I've met, did a great job as a tech editor. The quality and accuracy of this book is a testament to his thorough feedback.

Gordon Evans on the Salesforce.com staff was instrumental in getting us pointed in the right direction when we needed things along the way. Without Gordon's help, this book would have been a real chore, so thanks for everything, Gordon!

Thanks to my co-author Carol for not gloating too much when she finished her chapters early.

Kudos to Steve Stroz for stepping in to help us out. And of course, smooches to Kirsten.

Special thanks to Max Roach for letting me borrow my coauthors. Now that the book is done, you can have them back.

A big hug goes out to John for filling the void between chapters. Schelli and Aimee did wonders to keep me occupied during downtime. Hey Matt—give me a call about Salesforce. You all are great.

To my Global Services officemates: Courtney Fairchild, Jody Franklin, Matt Thompson, Martin, and whoever will replace Betty B. It's nice to know that I don't ever have to go farther than the rooftop desk of our office for a happy hour.

—EDWARD KACHINSKE

This is my first book with Edward, Stacy, and Tim. As the rookie on the team, I want to thank Edward and Stacy for their unfailing patience with me as I worked through style points, setup guides, and capturing screen images.

I also want to thank Jenny Davidson for her help as the project editor. She was totally on top of the deliverables and kept us on track, which I'm sure was hard at times—sort of like herding cats.

Special thanks for Ed Van Siclen at Salesforce.com in assisting to get us connected with the right people at Salesforce.com—Gordon and Brad have been great. Ethan Alexander, you saved my bacon at the very end—I owe you one!

—CAROL GILLILAND

This is my second book with Course Technology PTR, and it was a repeat of the wonderful experience I had the first time around. Working with Stacy Hiquet, Mitzi Koontz, and the whole team at Course Technology PTR was truly a pleasure.

Jenny Davidson, our project editor, deserves a medal for her humor and deft management of the entire process, and in particular her management of me!

To Ed Van Siclen at Salesforce.com—thanks for being willing to help and provide your opinion, especially since you are normally so shy and reserved.

To Brad for being an excellent and highly responsive resource for the technical editing; I could not have done my part without your support and help.

Thanks to my co-author Carol, for her wonderful support and encouragement. She called herself "The Rookie" in the process, yet, as always, she led the pack.

And to Edward Kachinske—once again, you have helped me though a really painful, yet powerful, learning curve and I am again in your debt for holding my hand throughout the process. It bears repeating that you are truly a rock star and I am a loyal and fanatical fan.

—STACY ROACH

About the Authors

Edward Kachinske is the author or co-author of 23 titles, including *Managing Contacts with Microsoft Outlook 2007 Business Contact Manager, Managing Contacts with ACT! 2005*, and *Managing Contacts with ACT! 2006.*

Edward has also published more than 100 articles in Customer Relationship Management (CRM) industry journals, and he is a primary author of more than 30 instructor-led training manuals for various CRM applications. Through print journals and electronic publications, more than a half-million people regularly read Edward's articles.

In his ten years in the industry, Edward has been a frequent speaker on contact management and customer relationship management subjects. Edward is the president of Innovative Solutions CRM, a firm that helps customers choose and implement CRM solutions with Salesforce, Microsoft applications, and Sage Software's CRM solutions.

Edward lives and works in Washington, DC.

Stacy Roach has over 18 years of sales and sales management experience. Her experience has primarily been in the technology industry and she is highly skilled at a variety of different selling strategies and techniques. She knows first-hand the value of using technology and tools to boost revenue and profits. She has personally relied on contact management tools to build strong relationships with her clients and manage her pipeline and forecasting.

Stacy was the co-author of *Managing Contacts with Microsoft Outlook 2007 Business Contact Manager* and has authored several articles for various Contact Management industry newsletters. She has presented and spoken at many contact management conferences. In 2001 Stacy, working with Edward Kachinske, started an annual conference, now called Mastering Small Business Consulting. The conference is geared toward CRM consulting firms that target the SMB market. The event attracts hundreds of consulting firm owners each year.

Stacy is a Managing Partner of Power of 3 Consulting, a firm that provides sales consulting and training, integrating their client's business process with contact management solutions. Stacy lives and works in the San Francisco Bay Area.

Carol Gilliland has held sales and sales management positions for almost 30 years. She began her career in advertising sales and then transitioned to consumer products, working for Procter & Gamble, a company that has always been highly regarded in hiring and training the best of the best. As technology became more accessible, she shifted gears into that industry and was a part of making high-tech products more consumer friendly.

Carol started her own business helping high-tech companies take their products to the retail channel. She assisted in channel development, messaging, package development, and price modeling. To ensure successful implementations, she developed and honed a practical business process.

She joined Power of 3 Consulting as a Managing Partner. In that role, she works with clients on their sales business process and leverages various sales tools, including Salesforce.com, in order to achieve their goals. Carol lives and works in the San Francisco Bay Area.

 Timothy Kachinske has authored more than a dozen titles in the CRM world, including *Managing Contacts with ACT! 2005* and *Managing Contacts with ACT! 2006*. He has published more than 150 industry-related articles, and he works as a contact management consultant.

Timothy lives in a suburb of Washington, DC, with his wife, Judith, and energetic West Highland Terrier, Harry. They have two sons.

Contents

Chapter 2
Working with Contacts 17

Chapter 3
Working with Leads 29

Chapter 4
Managing Opportunities and
Products 41

Chapter 5
List Views 73

Chapter 8
Writing Letters and Mail Merge 107

Chapter 9
Managing Documents 119

Chapter 10
Administering Campaigns...............127

Chapter 11
Reports & Dashboards 149

Chapter 12
Working with PDAs 167

Chapter 13
Working Offline..............................185

Chapter 16
Setting Up Your Database 213

Introduction

Salesforce.com is a web-based customer relationship management (CRM) tool, with many powerful and useful features for busy sales professionals. Folks in sales rarely have extra time to invest in learning a new application, even one that will help them better manage their relationships with their leads and customers. As a result, we designed this book to be used primarily as a reference tool. We have no illusions that this is a great cover-to-cover read. Our goal was to synthesize the primary functions of Salesforce used by most sales people, and present clear and concise instructions on those functions. You will be able to quickly and easily put your hands on the relevant information that you need and you won't have to sift through lots of superfluous content to get there.

The book is divided into chapters, and each chapter is divided into sections. Within each section, you'll find one or more tasks. Each page in this book covers a single task, and the tasks make up the bulk of the book. Salesforce.com offers six different versions, or editions. Each edition has user-level security that can be configured by your organization's Salesforce Administrator. At the end of each task, we indicate which edition that task applies to, and what specific security permissions you'll need to do that task. Since the people in sales are rarely also the application administrators, we did not include a whole lot of information on the setup and security functions. Salesforce provides online training and user support documents that do a pretty good job of presenting that information.

We have trained users on computer applications for over ten years and have found that people tend to both learn and retain computer skills best when they are hands-on, actually using the application. The tasks in this book are designed to walk you through the different functions of the application, step by step.

What Is Salesforce.com?

Salesforce.com is a web-based, customer-relationship management tool. There are six editions of Salesforce: Personal, Group, Professional, Enterprise, Unlimited, and Developer. Since the Personal edition can only have a single user, we don't cover it. Likewise, the Developer edition can only have two users, and it is designed for companies looking to develop add-on applications to extend Salesforce, so we don't include that edition either. This book deals with four editions: Group, Professional, Enterprise, and Unlimited.

All four of the editions we focus on provide the ability for sales professionals to manage their customer information and interactions, as well as follow up on sales leads and track sales opportunities. You can also manage documents; send template-based emails; integrate with Microsoft Outlook, Lotus Notes, and Microsoft Office; and you can even link a Google AdWords account to

Salesforce. All four editions reviewed in this book also provide dashboards to quickly view the information relevant to your business, as well as reports for analyzing data that are easy to use and customize for your needs. Depending on the edition, and sometimes for an additional fee, you can further extend Salesforce to include managing marketing campaigns, customer support, and workflow. You can also create a portal for partners or customers. And with the Salesforce AppExchange you have access to literally hundreds of add-on products to extend and further customize Salesforce for your organization.

If you are confused about the different Salesforce editions and the costs associated with the different options, well, you are not alone. We wish we could have you press your forehead to this page, think about what you really need and want from customer-relationship management software, and this page would magically display which version of Salesforce is right for your organization. But we couldn't figure out a way to make that happen. Our best advice is to read through this book, and pay attention to the functions you need for your business model. Then spend some time with others in your organization really analyzing your requirements for a CRM application, and compare your list against the features in Salesforce to see which edition gives you the most bang for your buck.

Chapter 1

Working with Accounts

- Adding and deleting accounts
- Viewing and printing account information
- Searching for accounts
- Sharing access to accounts
- Working with account teams

Adding and deleting accounts

In this section, you'll learn how to enter new accounts. Accounts are the top-level entity in Salesforce. Think of accounts as companies. Accounts are your customers. General Motors might be an account in your database, for example. You may then have contacts, opportunities, tasks, contracts, and more linked with the top-level account record.

Task A   Creating a new account

From just about anywhere in Salesforce, you can add a new account with the Create New drop-down.

To create a new account:

1. From the Create New drop-down on the left side of the Salesforce screen, choose the Account option.
2. Enter field information for your account.
3. Click the Save button.

In the Accounts tab, you can also click the New button to create a new account.

If your accounts already exist in a spreadsheet or other database, you can import them into Salesforce. Click the Accounts tab and then choose the Import My Accounts & Contacts option under the Tools header. Required fields are shown with a red bar to the left of the field.

To view accounts, you'll need **Read** permission on **Accounts**.

To create a new account, you'll need **Create** permission on **Accounts**.

This feature is available in:

✔ Unlimited   ✔ Developer
✔ Enterprise   ✔ Group
✔ Professional ✔ Personal

Task B Creating a sub account

General Motors is already in your database, but Pontiac is a division of General Motors. You can add Pontiac as a sub account under General Motors.

To add a division of an existing account:

1. Ensure that your parent company already exists as an account in Salesforce.
2. From the Create New drop-down on the left side of the Salesforce screen, choose the Account option.
3. Enter the name of the division in the Account Name field.
4. Next to the Parent Account field, click the magnifying glass icon.
5. Choose your parent company by clicking the name.
6. Enter any other information for your division.
7. Click Save.

To create a new division, you'll need **Create** permission on **Accounts**.

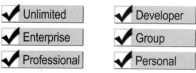

This feature is available in:

✔ Unlimited   ✔ Developer
✔ Enterprise   ✔ Group
✔ Professional ✔ Personal

Task C   Editing existing accounts

You may want to change information about one of your accounts. Editing an existing account is as easy as clicking the account's name in one of your lists of accounts.

Once you commit changes to an account, those edits cannot be undone.

To edit an account, you'll need **Edit** permission on **Accounts**.

To edit an existing account:

1. Click on the Accounts tab.
2. To find your contact, use the Search tool in the upper-left corner of the screen. Alternatively, you could browse one of your account views. Click the View drop-down at the top of the Accounts tab to browse through an account list.
3. When a list of accounts appears, click the name of the account.
4. Edit any information and click the Save button.

This feature is available in:

Unlimited   Developer
Enterprise   Group
Professional   Personal

Task D   Deleting an account

You may occasionally need to delete account records. You can do this in the Accounts tab, provided you have security permissions to delete accounts. Deleting an account will not delete any of the sub-accounts associated with the account. For example: General Motors is the parent account for Pontiac. If you delete General Motors, Pontiac will remain in the database.

To delete an account:

1. Click on the Accounts tab.
2. To find your contact, use the Search tool in the upper-left corner of the screen. Alternatively, you could browse one of your account views. Click the View drop-down at the top of the Accounts tab to browse through an account list.
3. When a list of accounts appears, click the name of the account. This brings up the account for editing.
4. Click the Delete button.
5. Click OK.

Deleted contacts are stored for a brief period in the Recycle Bin. Click the green Recycle Bin link on the left side of Salesforce.

To delete an account, you'll need **Delete** permission on **Accounts**.

This feature is available in:

✓ Unlimited   ✓ Developer

✓ Enterprise   ✓ Group

✓ Professional   ✓ Personal

Viewing and printing account information

Understanding how to view and print your account information is an important part of managing your sales with Salesforce. You can view accounts in one of the existing account lists, or you can create your own list.

Task A   Viewing account lists

Account lists show all of the accounts that match a set of predefined criteria. You can view all of your accounts, or you can view a subset of your Salesforce. Of course, the account lists will only display accounts that you have permission to see.

To view an account list:

1. Click on the Accounts tab.
2. At the top of the Accounts home page, click the View drop-down.
3. Click the account view that you would like to see. For example, you could click My Accounts to see a list of all accounts for whom you are the owner.

To jump to a specific spot in the list, click the letter of the alphabet that corresponds to the first letter of your company name. For example, if you were looking for XYZ Company, you would click the X in the alphabet at the top of the account list.

Click the Edit or Del links to the left of any account in an account list to either edit or delete the account.

To view an account list, you'll need **Read** permission on **Accounts**.

This feature is available in:

✔ Unlimited   ✔ Developer
✔ Enterprise   ✔ Group
✔ Professional   ✔ Personal

Task B   Creating a new account list

If you want to be able to easily bring up all of the accounts that match a certain criteria, you can create a new account list. Then, with only a click or two, you'll be able to view, edit, or print these accounts.

To create a new account list:

1. Click on the Accounts tab.
2. To the right of the View drop-down, click the Create New View link.
3. In Step 1, give your view a name.
4. In Step 2, you can filter to show just accounts that you own.
5. To add a field query for this view, add a field, operator, and value in the Filter By Additional Fields area. For example, if you wanted this view to just show contacts in Washington, DC, you'd choose: State as the field, equals as the operator, and DC as the value.
6. In Step 3, select the fields that you'd like to see displayed in the list view.
7. In Step 4, choose the users who should be able to see the view.
8. Click the Save button.

In Step 2 on the Salesforce screen, click the Advanced Options link to specify an advanced query for the filter. You would need to use this advanced query, for example, if you wanted to filter for all contacts in Maryland or Washington, DC.

To create a new account list, you'll need **Read** permission on **Accounts**.

To create a new public list view, you'll need **Manage Public List Views** permission.

Accounts
Create New View   Help for this Page

                        Save   Cancel

Step 1. Enter View Name | = Required Information

View Name: | Contacts in DC   (Example: "My Top Accounts")

Step 2. Specify Filter Criteria

Filter By Owner: Advanced Filters Help
  ⦿ All Accounts
  ○ My Accounts

Filter By Additional Fields (Optional):

Field	Operator	Value	
Billing State/Province	equals	DC	AND
--None--	--None--		AND
--None--	--None--		AND
--None--	--None--		AND
--None--	--None--		

Advanced Options...

Step 3. Select Fields to Display

This feature is available in:

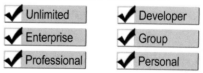

✔ Unlimited   ✔ Developer
✔ Enterprise   ✔ Group
✔ Professional   ✔ Personal

Task C   Viewing account hierarchy

You have both parent companies and divisions in your database. Sometimes, it can be really useful to see the account hierarchy because knowing who the parent company is might influence how you approach a sale.

To view the account hierarchy:

1. Click on the Accounts tab.
2. To find your contact, use the Search tool in the upper-left corner of the screen. Alternatively, you could browse one of your account views. Click the View drop-down at the top of the Accounts tab to browse through an account list.
3. When a list of accounts appears, click the name of the account.
4. Next to the Account Name, click the [View Hierarchy] link.
5. A list of subaccounts and parent companies for this account will appear. This hierarchical view shows all divisions under (and indented from) the parent company.

To view accounts, you'll need **Read** permission on **Accounts**.

To view parent accounts, you'll need **Read** permission on **Accounts**.

Account Hierarchy
sForce

Help for this Page

The hierarchy is created by associating accounts with parent accounts.

Account Name	Site	Type	Industry	Billing City	Billing State/Province	Owner
sForce				San Francisco	CA	Edward Kachinske
Acme Plubming						Edward Kachinske

This feature is available in:

✔ Unlimited   ✔ Developer
✔ Enterprise   ✔ Group
✔ Professional   ✔ Personal

Task D   Printing an account view

You have a set of accounts up on the screen, and Salesforce makes it really easy to print a list of these contacts. This is especially useful if you want to have basic contact information on a sheet of paper that you take out of the office.

To print an account view:

1. Click on the Accounts tab.
2. To find your contact, use the Search tool in the upper-left corner of the screen. Alternatively, you could browse one of your account views. Click the View drop-down at the top of the Accounts tab to browse through an account list.
3. When a list of accounts appears, click the name of the account.
4. In the upper-right corner of the screen, click the Printable View link. A printable screen will appear with account information, as well as basic contact information for linked contacts.
5. Click the Print This Page link to print or click the Print button on your web browser.

Instead of printing account information, you might be better served having information on your mobile device. See the chapter on Force.com mobile for help setting up Salesforce with your PDA. You can also send Salesforce contacts into Outlook or Lotus Notes.

To print an account view, you'll need **Read** permission on **Accounts**.

This feature is available in:

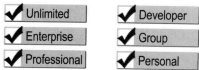

✔ Unlimited	✔ Developer
✔ Enterprise	✔ Group
✔ Professional	✔ Personal

Searching for accounts

Your data becomes a lot more valuable when you can find it! You can search for almost anything that has been entered for an account. In this section, you'll learn some core strategies for finding accounts in your Salesforce.

Task A   Finding a specific account

The boss wants you to work on the XYZ account. Your first step in researching XYZ is probably going to be to see if this account exists in Salesforce. Using these steps, you'll be able to go directly to the XYZ account record.

To find an account:

1. In the upper-left corner of the Accounts tab, click the Search All drop-down and choose the Accounts option.
2. Type the name of the company you'd like to find.
3. Click the Go! button.
4. A list of matching accounts appears.

Click the Advanced Search option to search for an exact phrase. In the Advanced Search area, you can also specify to search across multiple entities. For example, you could search across accounts, opportunities, tasks, and attachments for a word.

When searching for an account, you must know the first word in the Account Name field. Let's say you're looking for Acme Plumbing. You'd have to search for Acme, because searching for the word plumbing wouldn't yield any results.

To search for an account, you'll need **Read** permission on **Accounts**.

This feature is available in:

- ✔ Unlimited
- ✔ Developer
- ✔ Enterprise
- ✔ Group
- ✔ Professional
- ✔ Personal

Sharing access to accounts

In some cases, everyone in your organization will have access to all records. However, if you have divided your Salesforce by territory or other assignment, you'll need to know how to share access to account data.

Task A   Sharing accounts with others

The administrator sets global rules for sharing accounts, but you may want to change account sharing on an account-by-account basis. You can share an account with another user or a group of users. It's important to know that accounts (or person accounts, if you have that feature turned on) can be shared with other users. Contacts that are not associated with an account cannot be shared with others.

To share an account with other users:

1. Click on the Accounts tab.
2. To find your contact, use the Search tool in the upper-left corner of the screen. Alternatively, you could browse one of your account views. Click the View drop-down at the top of the Accounts tab to browse through an account list.
3. When a list of accounts appears, click the name of the account.
4. Click the Sharing button.
5. Click the Add button to add users or groups to the sharing list.

> **Sharing Detail**
> **Acme Plubming**   Help for this Page ?
>
> Acme Plubming
>
> Below is the list of users, groups and roles that have been granted sharing access to **Acme Plubming**. Click Expand List to view all users who have access to it.
>
> **User and Group Sharing** | Add | Expand List | User and Group Sharing Help ?
>
> | Action | Type | Name | Account Access | Opportunity Access | Case Access | Reason |
> |--------|------|------|----------------|--------------------|--------------|--------|
> | Edit | User | Edward Kachinske | Full Access | Private | Private | Owner |
> | Edit \| Del | User | John Smith | Read Only | Private | Private | Account Team |
>
> **Explanation of Access Levels**
> - Full Access - User can view, edit, delete, and transfer the record. User can also extend sharing access to other users.
> - Read/Write - User can view and edit the record, and add associated records, notes, and attachments to it.
> - Read Only - User can view the record, and add associated records to it. They cannot edit the record or add notes or attachments.
> - Private - User cannot access the record in any way.

If you do not have a Sharing button in the account editing screen, your organization may be configured so that all accounts are seen by all users. If this is the case, you don't get sharing options on individual accounts. (Because everyone can see that contact, there is no need to grant access to another user.)

🔒 To share access, you'll need **Edit** permission on **Accounts**.

🔒 Your ability to share also depends on your organization's sharing model.

This feature is available in:

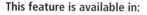

✔ Unlimited	✔ Developer
✔ Enterprise	Group
✔ Professional	Personal

Task B Changing account territories

If you use the territory feature in Salesforce, you can restrict access based on territory rules. A salesperson within your organization logs in and only sees accounts that are in his or her territory. This task shows you how to add an account to another territory.

To add an account to another territory:

1. Click on the Accounts tab.
2. To find your contact, use the Search tool in the upper-left corner of the screen. Alternatively, you could browse one of your account views. Click the View drop-down at the top of the Accounts tab to browse through an account list.
3. When a list of accounts appears, click the name of the account.
4. Click the Change link next to the Territories field.
5. Add this account to another territory from the list of available territories.
6. Click the Save button.

If you don't see a territory field in your account view, don't panic. Territory management must be enabled to assign an account to a territory. Ask your Salesforce administrator if you're unsure.

You can't remove an account from a territory if that territory membership is a result of your system-wide territory rules.

To change the territory of an account, you'll need **Manage Territories** permission.

Forecast Managers can also change territories.

This feature is available in:

✔ Unlimited	✔ Developer
✔ Enterprise	Group
Professional	Personal

Task C   Viewing the access list for an account

When you view the access list for an account, you'll see the list of users that have access to that account. Anyone with access to an account also has access to related information for the account—like contacts, notes, tasks, etc.

To view the access list for an account:

1. Click on the Accounts tab.
2. To find your contact, use the Search tool in the upper-left corner of the screen. Alternatively, you could browse one of your account views. Click the View drop-down at the top of the Accounts tab to browse through an account list.
3. When a list of accounts appears, click the name of the account.
4. Click the Sharing button.
5. Click the Expand List to see all of the users that have access to this account.

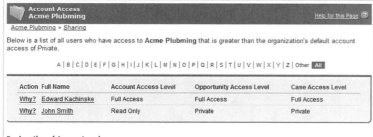

Access levels for a contact are:

- **Full Access:** This user can share the contact with other users and groups. Full access users can also transfer a contact.
- **Read/Write:** Read/Write users can view all aspects of an account, and they can add to or edit any part of the account.
- **Read Only:** Users can see the account and associated contacts, notes, etc. They can't make any changes, though.
- **Private:** If the user has private access, the account does not exist for this user.

To view the access list for an account, you'll need **Read** permission on **Accounts**.

This feature is available in:

Task D   Changing account ownership

If you want to transfer an account to another salesperson within your organization, you can change the ownership of the account. Of course, you'll need to have permission to change ownership to complete this task.

To change the ownership for an account:

1. Click on the Accounts tab.
2. To find your contact, use the Search tool in the upper-left corner of the screen. Alternatively, you could browse one of your account views. Click the View drop-down at the top of the Accounts tab to browse through an account list.
3. When a list of accounts appears, click the name of the account.
4. Next to the Account owner field, click the [Change] link.
5. Type the name of the new owner in the Owner field. (Or click the magnifying glass icon and choose from the list that appears.)
6. Select whether or not to transfer extra items, like open cases, closed opportunities, etc.
7. Click the Save button.

Oddly enough, once you've entered the edit page for an account, you can't change account ownership. The account owner field is only editable in the Account Detail page.

If you don't see a Change link, you probably don't have access to change the account's ownership.

To change account ownership of an account that you own, you'll need **Edit** permission on **Accounts**.

Ownership Edit
Acme Plubming   Help for this Page

This screen allows you to transfer an account from one user to another. When you transfer ownership of an account, the new owner will also gain ownership of the following records related to the transferred account:

- all notes and open activities for this account owned by you
- all contacts within the account owned by you, including all related notes and open activities owned by you
- all opportunities (including closed opportunities if you select the Transfer closed opportunities checkbox below) within the account owned by you, including all related notes and open activities owned by you

Note that completed activities will not be transferred.

The new owner might need to edit sharing.

Select New Owner | = Required Information

Transfer this account   Acme Plubming
Owner [   ]
☐ Transfer open opportunities not owned by the existing account owner
☐ Transfer closed opportunities
☐ Transfer open cases owned by the existing account owner
☐ Transfer closed cases
☐ Keep Account Team
☐ Send Notification Email

Save   Cancel

This feature is available in:

✔ Unlimited	✔ Developer
✔ Enterprise	✔ Group
✔ Professional	Personal

Working with account teams

If a number of users within your organization need access to a single account, you can set up an account team to manage access and responsibilities for the Salesforce users. Each account can have an account team.

Task A   Adding users to an account team

Your Salesforce administrator will create account teams for you. Adding users to an account team specifies what level of access the users have to your account. You can create a custom account team, or you can specify a default team.

To add users to an account team for an account:

1. Click on the Accounts tab.
2. To find your contact, use the Search tool in the upper-left corner of the screen. Alternatively, you could browse one of your account views. Click the View drop-down at the top of the Accounts tab to browse through an account list.
3. When a list of accounts appears, click the name of the account.
4. Scroll down to the Account Team related list and click the Add button.
5. Add team members, account/opportunity/case access levels, and team roles for each user in the team.
6. Click the Save button.

Account Team	Add	Add Default Team	Display Access	Delete All	Account Team Help
Action Team Member			Team Role		
Edit	Del John Smith			Account Manager		

You can configure your default account team by clicking Setup | My Personal Information | Personal Information.

The administrator defines the roles that you can specify for each user in the account team.

To add a user to an account team, you'll need **Edit** permission on **Accounts**.

This feature is available in:

15

Task B   Editing team members

As you change team membership for an account, the member users in your database will either gain or lose access to an account. If you don't own the account, you won't be able to edit team membership. See your Salesforce administrator for help if this is the case.

To edit team membership:

1. Click on the Accounts tab.
2. To find your contact, use the Search tool in the upper-left corner of the screen. Alternatively, you could browse one of your account views. Click the View drop-down at the top of the Accounts tab to browse through an account list.
3. When a list of accounts appears, click the name of the account.
4. Scroll down to the Account Team related list.
5. To remove someone from the team, click the Del link to the left of the user's name.
6. Click the Edit button to the left of the user's name to edit the specific access that this user has to the account.

Click the Display Access button to see what level of access each user has to accounts and opportunities/cases associated with the account.

To edit team members, you'll need **Edit** permission on **Accounts**.

This feature is available in:

✔ Unlimited	✔ Developer
✔ Enterprise	Group
Professional	Personal

Chapter 2

Working with Contacts

- Creating and editing contacts
- Viewing and finding contacts
- Stay-in-Touch Requests
- Searching for contacts
- Dealing with duplicates

Creating and editing contacts

A database is only as good as the data you've entered. In this section, you'll learn how to add new contacts to the database and enter information about these contacts. Salesforce is an account-centric system, so you might want to read the accounts chapter (Chapter 1) before browsing this chapter.

Task A   Creating a new contact

You can enter thousands (or hundreds of thousands) of contacts into Salesforce. Before entering a contact, you might use the search features to make sure the contact you are entering isn't a duplicate.

If you do not associate a contact with an account, the contact will be private. Private contacts cannot be included in reports, and they won't be viewable by other users.

To create a new contact, you'll need **Create** permission on **Contacts**.

To view contacts, you'll need **Read** permission on **Contacts**.

To create a new contact:

1. Click on the Contacts tab.
2. Click the New button in the Recent Contacts section to create a new contact. Alternatively, you could click the Create New drop-down on the left and choose the Contact option.
3. Enter a name (and any other information) for your contact.
4. You should also associate the contact with an account. Click the magnifying glass icon next to the Account field to choose from a list of existing accounts.
5. Click the Save button.

This feature is available in:

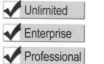

✔ Unlimited   ✔ Developer

✔ Enterprise   ✔ Group

✔ Professional ✔ Personal

Task B Editing an existing contact

You can edit an existing contact just by clicking on the name of the contact in any list view.

To edit an existing contact:

1. Click on the Contacts tab.
2. In the upper-left corner of the screen, use the Search area to find a specific contact. Alternatively, you could click a view from the View drop-down at the top of the Contacts tab.
3. Browse through your view (or search results) until you find the contact you'd like to edit.
4. Click the name of the contact to bring up contact details.
5. Click the Edit button to edit any field information for the contact. You can also edit much of the information inline.

Even if you have the default Edit permission on contacts, you'll need to have access to a contact to edit it. Ask your administrator for help if you don't see the option to edit a contact.

To edit an existing contact, you'll need **Edit** permission on **Contacts**.

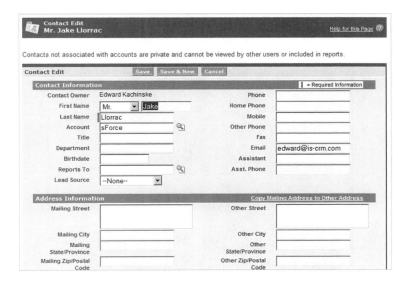

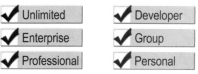

Task C   Deleting a contact

Deleting an unwanted contact is just as simple as adding a new one. Be careful when deleting contacts, though. If you accidentally delete a contact, it only sits in the Recycle Bin for 30 days.

Deleted items live in the Recycle Bin for 30 days or until you reach your Recycle Bin capacity limit. The capacity limit is 250x your data storage limit. So, if you have capacity for 2MB of data storage, you could have 500MB of data in your Recycle Bin.

To delete contacts, you'll need **Delete** permission on **Contacts**.

To delete a contact:

1. Click on the Contacts tab.
2. In the upper-left corner of the screen, use the Search area to find a specific contact. Alternatively, you could click a view from the View drop-down at the top of the Contacts tab.
3. Browse through your view (or search results) until you find the contact you'd like to delete.
4. Click the name of the contact to bring up details for the contact record.
5. Click the Delete button.
6. Click OK to confirm.

> The page at https://na5.salesforce.com says:
>
> ? Are you sure?
>
> OK   Cancel

This feature is available in:

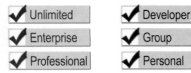

✔ Unlimited   ✔ Developer
✔ Enterprise   ✔ Group
✔ Professional   ✔ Personal

Viewing and finding contacts

In the Contacts view, you can browse through all of your contacts. You can also search for a specific contact or create a view of contacts that matches set criteria.

| Task A | Viewing contact lists |

Understanding contact list views is an important part of navigating through your large list of contacts. A contact list view is a set of contacts—predetermined by a query that you set—that is easily brought up from the Contacts tab.

To view a contact list:

1. Click on the Contacts tab.
2. In the View drop-down, select a view from your list of predefined contact list views.
3. Click the Go! button. A list of all contacts that match the view's predefined query will appear.

Click the Edit link next to the View drop-down to edit an existing view, or click the Create New View link to create a new view from scratch.

To view a contact list, you'll need **Read** permission on **Contacts**.

This feature is available in:

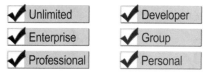

✔ Unlimited   ✔ Developer

✔ Enterprise   ✔ Group

✔ Professional   ✔ Personal

Task B Printing contact information

If you bring up a list of all contacts with a birthday this month, you may want to print the list so you can call people while you're out of the office. You may just want a list of contact information for your next meeting. You can use the Printable View feature to print information for a single contact or multiple contacts.

To print information for a contact:

1. Click on the Contacts tab.
2. From the View drop-down, choose the contact list you'd like to view.
3. Click the Go! button.
4. Your contact list will appear. In the upper-right corner of the view, click the Printable view link.
5. If you want detailed information on a specific contact, click the name of the contact to bring up contact details.
6. In the contact details area, you'll see the same Printable View link in the upper-right corner.

If you need to print more than a page or two of contacts, you should probably use reports to get the data on paper. Chapter 11 covers the reporting features in Salesforce.

To print a screen, you'll need **Read** permission on **Contacts**.

This feature is available in:

- ✔ Unlimited
- ✔ Enterprise
- ✔ Professional
- ✔ Developer
- ✔ Group
- ✔ Personal

Task C   Viewing contact hierarchy

John Smith reports to Jane Doe, and they both work for ABC Company. Understanding the hierarchy within the ABC Company will help you know which person to contact in a situation. For any contact in Salesforce, you can see the contact within its company's organizational chart.

To view a contact's hierarchy:

1. Click on the Contacts tab.
2. In the upper-left corner of the screen, use the Search area to find a specific contact. Alternatively, you could click a view from the View drop-down at the top of the Contacts tab.
3. Browse through your view (or search results) until you find the contact whose organizational chart you'd like to see. Click the name of the contact to bring up its details.
4. Click the View Org Chart link next to the Reports To field.
5. An org chart for this contact (and his/her colleagues) will appear.

> **Org Chart**
> **Betty Smith**   Help for this Page
>
> Salesforce creates an organization chart based on the contacts selected in the Reports To field of each contact. To create a single chart for an account, make sure every contact but the one at the top of the hierarchy contains another contact in the Reports To field.
>
> **Name**
>
> ⊟ Jake Llorrac
>   ⊟ John Smith
>   └ Betty Smith

Salesforce uses a combination of the Reports To field and the contact/account association to create the organizational hierarchy. If you haven't linked your contacts with accounts, and if you haven't filled information into the Reports To field, the organizational chart probably won't be accurate.

To view a contact's organizational chart, you'll need **Read** permission on **Contacts**.

To edit a contact's organizational chart, you'll need **Edit** permission on **Contacts**.

This feature is available in:

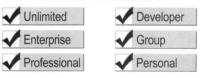

✔ Unlimited	✔ Developer
✔ Enterprise	✔ Group
✔ Professional	✔ Personal

Stay-in-Touch requests

The Stay-in-Touch feature makes it easy for you to get updated contact information for people in your Salesforce system. You can send individual Stay-in-Touch requests, and you can also send a mass Stay-in-Touch email.

Task A   Request updated information for a contact

Anytime you are looking at the details of a contact, you can click the Request Update button at the top of the contact detail screen to send an email to the contact requesting updated contact info.

To send a Stay-in-Touch request to a single contact:

1. Click on the Contacts tab.
2. In the upper-left corner of the screen, use the Search area to find a specific contact. Alternatively, you could click a view from the View drop-down at the top of the Contacts tab.
3. Browse through your view (or search results) until you find the contact for whom you'd like to request updated information.
4. Click the name of the contact to bring up details for the contact record.
5. Click the Request Update button at the top of the contact detail screen.
6. Check the contents of your Stay-in-Touch request. Make any changes to the message and click Send.

You can only request updated information for contacts that have an email address.

To send Stay-in-Touch requests, you'll need **Send Stay-in-Touch Requests** permission.

This feature is available in:

✔ Unlimited   ✔ Developer
✔ Enterprise   ✔ Group
✔ Professional   ✔ Personal

Task
Send a Stay-in-Touch Request   Help for this Page

[Send] [Check Spelling] [Cancel]

To request updated information from your contact, edit the form below. Use the Mass Stay-in-Touch tool on The contact Home page if you'd like to update many contacts at once.

Last Stay-in-Touch Request

Last Stay-in-Touch Save

You can customize the note and signature for Stay-in-Touch emails in the Stay-In-Touch settings page.

Edit Email | = Required Information

To   John Smith
CC
BCC
Subject   Staying in touch
Note   Hi John,

            I'm updating my address book and I want to be sure we keep in touch. Can you take a look at the info I have for you below and let me know if it's out of date?

Task B   Request updated information from multiple contacts

If you found the previous task useful, you'll love the ability to send a Stay-in-Touch request to multiple contacts. Running this task sends an email to multiple contacts in your database asking them to verify or update the contact information you have in Salesforce.

To request updated information from multiple contacts:

1. Click on the Contacts tab.
2. In the Tools section, click the Mass Stay-in-Touch option.
3. Select the view that contains the recipients to be included in the email.
4. Click the name of the contact to bring up details for the contact record.
5. Click the Go! button.
6. Verify your recipients and click the Next button.
7. Verify the contents of the Stay-in-Touch email.
8. Click the Send button.

Before you send a mass Stay-in-Touch request, make sure you have created a view that contains all of the people who should get the Stay-in-Touch email. To create a new view, click the Create New View link in the Contacts tab.

To send Stay-in-Touch requests, you'll need **Send Stay-in-Touch Requests** permission.

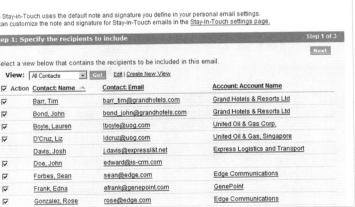

This feature is available in:

✓ Unlimited	✓ Developer
✓ Enterprise	✓ Group
✓ Professional	✓ Personal

Searching for contacts

You can add a million contacts to your Salesforce, but doing so doesn't do much good if you can't find them. In this section, we'll cover some basic techniques for finding specific contacts. You should probably also familiarize yourself with the chapter on list views (Chapter 5), since traditional advanced queries (the kind with Boolean operators) are achieved in Salesforce by creating contact lists.

Task A   Finding a specific contact

Betty Smith is on the phone. She's very important, and she's talking about a million-dollar deal. You have no idea who she is. You only have about ten seconds before she realizes this. Luckily, a log of everything your company has done with her is in Salesforce. You should be able to find her record within ten seconds.

To find a specific contact:

1. In the upper-left corner of most Salesforce screens, locate the gray search area. (If you don't see it, click the Contacts tab and it should appear.)
2. In the Search drop-down, choose the Contacts option.
3. Enter the contact's first name, last name, or both.
4. Click the Go! button.
5. All of the matching contacts will appear. Click the name of the person whose information you'd like to see.

When you are searching, click the Limit to items I own checkmark to only look through the contacts that have you listed as the record owner.

To search for a contact, you'll need **Read** permission on **Contacts**.

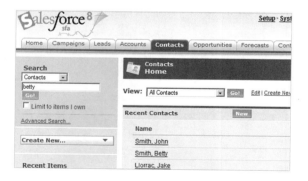

This feature is available in:

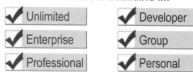

✔ Unlimited   ✔ Developer
✔ Enterprise   ✔ Group
✔ Professional ✔ Personal

Dealing with duplicates

Duplicates are an undesired part of any database. Within your list of contacts, duplicates can be especially menacing. If a customer exists in your database twice, it might mean that two different people from your organization are actively pursuing the lead.

Task A	Merging duplicate contacts

Salesforce has a feature that helps you identify duplicate records. This process assumes that the duplicate contacts are both associated with the same account record.

To find duplicate contacts:

1. Click on the Accounts tab.
2. Click the name of any account to bring up details for that account.
3. Scroll down to the Contacts related list.
4. Click the Merge Contacts button.
5. Check all of the contacts that should be merged.
6. Click Next.
7. Select a master record. If any data from a non-master contact should be retained, check the radio button next to the field that should be retained.
8. Click Merge.

Contacts		New	Merge Contacts			Contacts Help
Action	Contact Name		Title	Email	Phone	
Edit | Del	John Doe					
Edit | Del	John Doe				(415) 901-7000	
Edit | Del	Jake Llorrac			edward@is-crm.com		
Edit | Del	Siddartha Nedaerk					

To find duplicates, you'll need **Read** permission on **Contacts**.

This feature is available in:

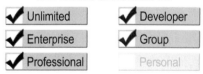

✔ Unlimited   ✔ Developer

✔ Enterprise   ✔ Group

✔ Professional   Personal

Chapter 3

Working with Leads

- Lead basics
- Sharing access to leads
- Dealing with duplicates
- Converting leads

Lead basics

Leads are tadpoles; contacts are frogs. If the person you are entering into the database is a potential customer, enter this person as a lead. Then, when the contact becomes an actual customer, you can convert the lead to a contact.

Task A   Entering a new lead

When a prospective customer calls, you will want to record his or her information somewhere. Enter this prospective customer as a lead into Salesforce.

To enter a new lead:

1. Click on the Leads tab.
2. Click the Create New drop-down and choose the Lead option. Alternatively, you could click the New button in the Leads home page.
3. Enter all of the contact information for this lead and click the Save button.

Overwhelmed by the thought of typing in all of your leads manually? Use the Web-to-Lead feature. Click Setup | Customize | Leads | Web to Lead. This feature allows you to capture information that your customers enter on a website, and this information flows directly into Salesforce in the form of a lead.

Lead defaults can be configured by clicking Setup | Customize | Leads | Settings.

🔒 To view leads, you'll need **Read** permission on **Leads**.

🔒 To enter a new lead, you'll need **Create** permission on **Leads**.

This feature is available in:

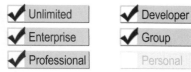

✔ Unlimited	✔ Developer
✔ Enterprise	✔ Group
✔ Professional	Personal

Task B   Finding leads

As a salesperson, one of the most useful components of Salesforce is its ability to quickly bring up a list of leads. Need to know who your hot prospects are? Have some free time at the end of the day when you'd like to sell something? Take a look at your lead list.

To view or edit a lead:

1. Click on the Leads tab.
2. You can search for a specific lead, or click the View drop-down to view a list of leads. You may also find the lead you're looking for in the Recent Leads list.
3. Locate your lead and click the name of the lead to bring up details for the lead.
4. Click the Edit button to change any information for the lead.

Related Lists: While you are viewing a lead, scroll down to see related lists of information about your leads. Related lists help you understand the current state of your leads by showing associated activities, notes, campaigns, etc.

Click the Printable View button in the upper-right corner of any lead screen to print the information on the page.

To view leads, you'll need **Read** permission on **Leads**.

To edit leads, you'll need **Edit** permission on **Leads**.

This feature is available in:

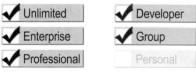

Task C   Cloning leads

You're selling one product to a person at XYZ Company. At the same time, your contact at XYZ Company refers you to another person at XYZ who might be interested in one of your services. Cloning the first lead will save you the trouble of re-typing shared basic contact information—like the company name, address, and main telephone number.

To clone a lead, you'll need **Create** permission on **Leads**.

To clone a lead:

1. Click on the Leads tab.
2. Locate your lead and click the name of the lead to bring up details for the lead.
3. Click the Edit button to edit properties for the lead.
4. Click the Clone button.
5. Change any information for the cloned lead and click Save.

Lead					
Ms Kristen Akin				Printable View | Custo	
« Back to List: Leads					
Open Activities [0] | Activity History [0] | Campaign History [0] | HTML Email St					
Lead Detail		Edit	Delete	Convert	Clone	Find Duplicates
Lead Owner	Edward Kachinske [Change]		Phone	(434) 36	
Name	Ms Kristen Akin		Mobile		
Company	Aethna Home Products		Fax		
Title	Director, Warehouse Mgmt		Email	kakin@a	
Lead Source	Partner Referral		Website		
Industry			Lead Status	Working	
Annual Revenue			Rating		
			No. of Employees		
Address					

This feature is available in:

✔ Unlimited   ✔ Developer
✔ Enterprise   ✔ Group
✔ Professional   Personal

Task D Viewing history of a lead

There's a lead in Salesforce. You're looking at it, and you can't remember if this is someone you have spoken with. You don't know if it is a person who has been contacted by one of your colleagues. Before calling a lead, take a look at the history of the lead to see what activities, campaigns, and emails have been associated with the person.

To view the history of a lead:

1. Click on the Leads tab.
2. Click on the name of a lead. You may need to go into one of your lead list views to see the lead.
3. When the lead comes up on the screen, scroll down to see open activities, activity history, campaign history, and email status for this lead.

Click the Printable View link in the upper-right corner of the lead to print a quick report that shows basic field information for your lead, as well as details of the lead history.

To view lead history, you'll need **Read** permission on **Leads**.

Open Activities		New Task	New Event				Open Activities Help
Action	Subject	Task	Due Date	Status	Priority	Assigned To	
Edit | Cls	stuff	✓		Not Started	Normal	Edward Kachinske	
Edit | Cls	Doohickey	✓		Not Started	Normal	Edward Kachinske	
Edit | Cls	Send her a letter	✓		Not Started	Normal	Edward Kachinske	

Activity History		Log A Call	Mail Merge	Send An Email	View All	Activity History Help
Action	Subject	Task	Due Date	Assigned To	Last Modified Date/Time	
Edit | Del	Email: hey	✓	3/16/2008	Edward Kachinske	3/16/2008 9:42 PM	
Edit | Del	Call	✓	3/16/2008	Edward Kachinske	3/16/2008 9:42 PM	

Campaign History		Add Campaign					Campaign History Help
Action	Campaign Name		Start Date	Type	Status	Responded	Member Status Updated
Edit | Del	DM Campaign to Top Customers - Nov 12-23, 2001		11/12/2001	Direct Mail	Sent		3/16/2008 9:42 PM

HTML Email Status		Send An Email	View All			HTML Email Status Help
Action	Subject	Date Sent	Date Opened	# Times Opened	Last Opened	
Edit | Del	Email: hey	3/16/2008 9:42 PM		0		

This feature is available in:

✔ Unlimited	✔ Developer
✔ Enterprise	Group
Professional	Personal

Task E   Deleting a lead

If a lead is no longer needed, or if you realized after entering a lead that it already existed in Salesforce, you can delete the lead.

Deleted leads are moved to the Recycle Bin.

To delete leads, you'll need **Delete** permission on **Leads**.

To delete a lead:

1. Click on the Leads tab.
2. Click the name of a lead to open details for the lead.
3. Click the Delete button to delete the lead.

The page at https://na5.salesforce.com says:

Are you sure?

OK   Cancel

This feature is available in:

✔ Unlimited   ✔ Developer

✔ Enterprise   ✔ Group

✔ Professional   Personal

Sharing access to leads

During lunchtime, you answered the phone. It was a prospective customer, and you entered this person's information as a lead in Salesforce. It's not your lead, though, and Salesforce lets you assign this lead to another user in your workgroup.

Task A Changing lead ownership

You can assign leads to other users, groups, or queues. If you assign a lead to another user, the lead will show up in his or her list of leads. If you own the lead, it's easy to assign it to someone else.

To change ownership for a lead:

1. Click on the Leads tab.
2. Click the name of a lead you'd like to assign. This brings up the details for the lead.
3. Click the [Change] link next to the Lead Owner field.
4. You can transfer this link to either another user or a lead queue. Select User or Queue from the Owner drop-down.
5. Click the magnifying glass icon next to the Owner field and choose a new owner or queue.
6. Click Save.

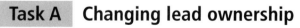

This screen allows you to transfer ownership of a lead to another user or queue. When you transfer ownership of a lead, the new owner will own:
- all notes and attachments recorded for the current owner
- all open activities (tasks and events) owned by the current owner

Note that completed activities and open activities owned by other users will not be transferred.

Select New Owner

Transfer this lead   Ms Kristen Akin
Owner [User ▾] [   ] 🔍
☐ Send Notification Email

[Save] [Cancel]

When importing leads into Salesforce, or when using the Web-to-Lead feature, your administrator can set assignment rules to automatically distribute leads. If you are the Minnesota rep, any Minnesota lead imported will automatically show up assigned to you.

The Salesforce administrator in your company can define the lead distribution settings. The tasks on this page show you how to manually assign a lead to a user.

To reassign a lead, you'll need **Read** and **Edit** permission on **Leads**.

This feature is available in:

Unlimited ✔   Developer ✔
Enterprise ✔   Group
Professional   Personal

Task B Changing ownership for multiple leads

If you want to assign multiple leads to another user, you can do it from within any of the lead list views.

To change ownership for multiple leads:

1. Click on the Leads tab.
2. Choose a list view from the View drop-down.
3. Click the checkbox field next to each lead whose ownership should be changed.
4. Click the Change Owner button.
5. Click the magnifying glass icon next to the Owner field and choose a new owner.
6. Click Save.

Click the Edit link next to any lead to change details for the lead.

To mass transfer leads, go to the Leads home page and click the Mass Transfer Leads link. Here, you can transfer all leads that meet specific criteria to another user.

To reassign a lead, you'll need **Read** and **Edit** permission on **Leads**.

All Open Leads					

View: All Open Leads ▼ Edit | Create New View

A | B | C | D | E | F | G | H | I | J | K | L | M | N | O | P | Q | R | S | T | U | V | W | X | Y |

				Change Status	Change Owner	Add to Campaign

☑ Action	Name ∧	Company	State/Province	Email	Lead Status
☑ Edit Del	Akin, Kristen	Aethna Home Products	VA	kakin@athenahome.com	Working - Contacted
☑ Edit Del	Bair, Betty	American Banking Corp.	PA	bblair@abankingco.com	Working - Contacted
☑ Edit Del	Boxer, Bertha	Farmers Coop. of Florida	FL	bertha@fcof.net	Working - Contacted
☑ Edit Del	Braund, Mike	Metropolitan Health Services	MD	likeb@metro.com	Open - Not Contacted
☑ Edit Del	Brownell, Shelly	Western Telecommunications Corp.	CA	shellyb@westerntelecom.com	Working - Contacted
☑ Edit Del	Cotton, Phyllis	Abbott Insurance	VA	pcotton@abbottins.net	Open - Not Contacted
☑ Edit Del					Open - Not

This feature is available in:

✔ Unlimited   ✔ Developer
✔ Enterprise   Group
  Professional   Personal

Dealing with duplicates

Duplicates are an undesired part of any database. Within your list of leads, duplicates can be especially menacing. If a potential customer exists in your database twice, it might mean that two different people from your organization are actively pursuing the lead.

Task A Finding duplicate leads

Salesforce has a feature that helps you identify duplicate records. While it isn't 100% accurate, it is a good first step in your de-duplication process. Unfortunately, it would be nearly impossible to program a button that would—with a single click—remove all of your duplicates with 100% accuracy. Any duplicate merging system ends up requiring a certain amount of human interaction.

To find duplicate leads:

1. Click on the Leads tab.
2. Click the name of any lead to bring up details for that lead.
3. Click the Find Duplicates button.
4. In the top part of the screen, check the fields you'd like to use to search for duplicate leads.
5. Click Search. A list of leads matching the fields you selected in step 4 will appear below.

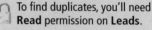

To find duplicates, you'll need **Read** permission on **Leads**.

Lead
Betty Bair - Search for Duplicates

Help for this Page

| Search | Convert Lead | Cancel |

Name	☑	Betty Bair
Last Name	☐	Bair
Company	☑	American Banking Corp
Email	☑	bblair@abankingco.com
Email Domain	☐	@abankingco.com
Phone	☑	(610) 265-9100

| Search | Convert Lead | Cancel |

Matching Leads   Merge Leads

☐	Name	Title	Phone	Company	Email	Lead Status	Owner Alias
☐	Ms Betty Bair	VP, Administration	(610) 265-9100	American Banking Corp.	bblair@abankingco.com	Working - Contacted	EKach
☐	Ms Betty Bair	VP, Administration	(610) 265-9100	American Banking Corp.	bblair@abankingco.com	Working - Contacted	EKach

This feature is available in:

✔ Unlimited   ✔ Developer
✔ Enterprise   ✔ Group
✔ Professional   Personal

Task B Merging duplicate leads

When merging duplicate leads, basic field information will be taken from your duplicate records and merged into one final record. Related lists—like notes and attachments—are also merged into this final record. Once all information has been sent over to the final contact, the original duplicates are deleted from Salesforce.

To merge duplicate leads:

1. Follow all of the steps from Task A on the preceding page.
2. If you see duplicate lead records in the Matching Leads page, check each lead in your duplicate group.
3. Click the Merge Leads button.
4. Choose a Master Record, and where information differs between your two leads, select the data you'd like to keep in the final lead.
5. Click the Merge button.
6. Click OK.

You can merge up to three duplicate (or triplicate) contacts. If you have four instances in the database of the same person, you'll have to run the duplicate merging process multiple times to fully eradicate the duplicate records.

Merging cannot be undone.

To merge duplicates, you'll need **Delete** permission on **Leads**.

Merge Leads   Help for this Page

[Previous] [Merge] [Cancel]

Select the values that you want to retain in the merged record. Highlighted rows indicate fields that contain conflicting data. The Master Record selected will retain read-only and hidden field values. The oldest Created By date and user will be retained in the merged record.

Note: All related records including any campaigns and activities will be associated with the new merged record.

	Ms Betty Bair [Select All]	Ms Betty Bair [Select All]
Master Record	⦿	○
Lead Owner	Edward Kachinske	Edward Kachinske
Name	Ms Betty Bair	Ms Betty Bair
Company	American Banking Corp.	American Banking Corp.
Title	VP, Administration	VP, Administration
Lead Source	Purchased List	Purchased List
Campaign		
Industry		
Annual Revenue		
Phone	(610) 265-9100	(610) 265-9100
Mobile		
Fax		
Email	bblair@abankingco.com	bblair@abankingco.com
Website		
Lead Status	Working - Contacted	Working - Contacted
Rating		
No. of Employees		
Address		
	PA	PA
	USA	USA
Product Interest	GC5000 series	GC5000 series
SIC Code	2768	2768
Number of Locations	130	130

This feature is available in:

✔ Unlimited   ✔ Developer
✔ Enterprise   ✔ Group
✔ Professional   Personal

Converting leads

Once your lead becomes a qualified lead or an actual customer, you can convert the lead to a contact, account, opportunity, or task. After converting a lead, information from the lead—like the name, address, and other data—is sent over to a new record and the original lead is removed from the lead list. A lead becomes a contact, which can be associated with an account or opportunity.

Task A   Converting a lead

When converting a lead to an account/opportunity, you will have an opportunity to change some last-minute details, like the record owner.

To convert a lead to an account:

1. Click on the Leads tab.
2. Click on a lead to bring up details for the lead.
3. Click the Convert button.
4. If you would like to add an opportunity for the new account, enter the name of the opportunity in the Opportunity Name field. If not, click the Do not create a new opportunity upon conversion option.
5. Select a status for the opportunity, if you are creating an opportunity.
6. If you would like to create a follow-up task for this account, enter details into the Task Information area.
7. Click the Convert button.

To convert leads, you'll need:

- **Convert Leads** permission.
- **Create** permission on **Leads**.
- **Edit** permission on **Leads**.
- **Create** permission on **Contacts**.
- **Edit** permission on **Contacts**.
- **Create** permission on **Accounts**.
- **Edit** permission on **Accounts**.
- **Create** permission on **Opportunities**.
- **Edit** permission on **Opportunities**.

Convert Lead
Betty Bair   Help for this Page ⊘

Leads can be converted to accounts, contacts, opportunities, and followup tasks.
You should only convert a lead once you have identified it as qualified.
After this lead has been converted, it can no longer be viewed or edited as a lead, but can be viewed in lead reports.

[Convert] [Cancel]

Convert Lead | = Required Information

Record Owner	Edward Kachinske 🔍
Send Email to the Owner	☐
Account Name	Create New Account: American Banking Corp.
Opportunity Name	American Banking Corp
	☐ Do not create a new opportunity upon conversion.
Converted Status	Closed - Converted ▾

Task Information

Subject		Status	Not Started ▾
Due Date	[3/16/2008]		
Priority	Normal ▾		

Description Information

Comments

☐ Send Notification Email

This feature is available in:

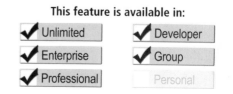

✔ Unlimited   ✔ Developer
✔ Enterprise   ✔ Group
✔ Professional   Personal

Chapter 4

Managing Opportunities and Products

- ■ Working with opportunities
- ■ Viewing and monitoring opportunities
- ■ Managing products
- ■ Managing price books
- ■ Managing your sales forecast

Working with opportunities

Tracking your sales opportunities is one of the most powerful functions of Salesforce. You can create and track an opportunity as it moves through the sales cycle. You can also link activities, contacts, partners, competitors, history, and notes and attachments to the opportunity. You can associate opportunities with specific marketing campaigns to track the effectiveness and the ROI on campaigns. Managing your opportunities and all the related information provides excellent visibility into your sales cycle, and a great tool to help you sell more effectively.

Task A   Creating an opportunity

Creating an opportunity in Salesforce is a simple task. You can either create a new opportunity from the Opportunity home view or click in the Create New drop-down in the left sidebar, and select Opportunity.

To create a new opportunity:

1. Click on the Opportunities tab to go to the Opportunities home view.
2. Click on the Create New button in the left sidebar and choose Opportunity.
3. Fill in the opportunity information in the Opportunity Edit screen. Note that all required information will be indicated with a red vertical bar next to the field.
4. You can associate an opportunity with an account by clicking on the Account Name Lookup icon to the left of the Account Name field.
5. You can associate an opportunity with a campaign by clicking on the Campaign Lookup icon to the left of the Campaign Source field.
6. When you are finished entering the basic opportunity information, click the Save button at the bottom of the Opportunity Edit screen.

Your company's Salesforce system administrator can customize the new opportunity screen, adding fields that are relevant to your business model. He can also determine which of the fields in the opportunity screen are required. You cannot save a new opportunity until you have filled in all the required fields.

If your company has enabled the Quick Create function in Salesforce then you will see a Quick Create box in the left sidebar on the Opportunity home page. You can enter the name of an opportunity; associate it with an account; and put in the expected close date, current stage, and amount. Note that the opportunity name, close date, and stage are all required fields in the Quick Create box, as indicated by a red asterisk. Also, the date field here does not bring up a nice calendar pop-up, but instead you must manually type in the date, and it must be in this format: mm/dd/yy.

To view opportunities, you'll need **Read** permission on **Opportunities**.

To create opportunities, you'll need **Create** permission on **Opportunities**.

This feature is available in:

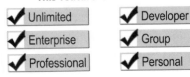

✔ Unlimited   ✔ Developer
✔ Enterprise   ✔ Group
✔ Professional   ✔ Personal

Task B   Adding products to an opportunity

Once you have created an opportunity, you can add multiple products to that opportunity to track the specific items that make up that opportunity. Your administrator will set up products and pricebooks for your organization.

To add products to an opportunity:

1. If you just created the opportunity, when you click Save you will be taken to the Opportunity Detail view, where you can view and add products.
2. In the Products area, click the Add Product button. If your organization has more than one price book, select the Price Book from the drop-down and click Save. For more information on price books, see the section on managing products in this chapter.
3. You can select a product by clicking in the check box to the left of the product, then clicking Select.
4. Enter the quantity for the product(s) and the sales price. If you have enabled schedules for your products, you can also set the schedule date by product.
5. Click Save.

Add Products to Huge Deal

Add products to this opportunity from **Standard Price Book** price book.

		Save	Save & More	Cancel		
Product	Quantity		Sales Price	Date [3/22/2008]	Line Description	
Sales Process Review	1		25,000.00	4/30/2008		
		Save	Save & More	Cancel		

There is a feature your company can configure so that when you add a new opportunity, you can click Save & Add Product to go directly to the Product Selection view. Enabling that feature will save you a few clicks when creating a new opportunity. Contact your administrator for more information.

If your organization has set up multiple price books, for different product lines or divisions, for example, you will first need to select the price book before adding products to an opportunity. You cannot mix products from multiple price books in one opportunity though, and if you change the price book on an existing opportunity, Salesforce will delete all of the products selected from the previous price book for that opportunity.

To view opportunity products, you'll need **Read** permission on **Opportunities**, **Products**, and **Price Books**.

To edit opportunity products, you'll need **Edit** permission on **Opportunities**.

This feature is available in:

✔ Unlimited	✔ Developer
✔ Enterprise	✔ Group
✔ Professional	✔ Personal

Task C   Creating an opportunity from an account

Opportunities can be associated with an account or a contact. You can associate an opportunity with a specific account by simply creating the new opportunity from the account record.

To create an opportunity from an account:

1. Click the Accounts tab, search for the account, and then select the account by clicking on the account name. You will now be in the Account Detail view.
2. Click on the Create New button on the left sidebar and choose Opportunity.
3. Fill in the opportunity information in the Opportunity Edit screen and click Save.
4. Add products to the opportunity and click Save.
5. Click on the Opportunity detail view; the account you selected will be indicated next to Account Name.

If you are adding or editing an account, you can easily create a new opportunity from the Account view, which will associate that opportunity with the account you were working with, saving you the step of searching for an account when creating an opportunity.

To create opportunities, you'll need **Create** permission on **Opportunities**.

To view opportunity products, you'll need **Read** permission on **Opportunities**, **Products**, and **Price Books**.

To edit opportunity products, you'll need **Edit** permission on **Opportunities**.

This feature is available in:

✔ Unlimited   ✔ Developer

✔ Enterprise   ✔ Group

✔ Professional   ✔ Personal

Task D Assigning contact roles in an opportunity

There are likely several people involved in any opportunity. Identifying the players and their role is key to moving the sale forward and closing the deal. Salesforce provides a great tool for identifying the specific individuals related to an opportunity, defining the primary contact, as well as other involved contacts and their roles. You want to be working with the decision maker, but you also need to know any influencers, obstacles, financial decision makers, etc. that can have an impact on your ability to win that opportunity.

To assign contact roles in an opportunity:

1. Click in the Opportunities tab to go to the Opportunities home view.
2. Find the opportunity for which you want to edit the contacts and roles, and click on the opportunity name to go to the Opportunity Detail screen.
3. In the Contact Roles section, click New.
4. Click the Contact Lookup icon to the right of the field for the contact name.
5. Search for the contact you want to associate with this opportunity, and then click on the contact's name to add her to the opportunity.
6. Assign the role that this contact will play in the opportunity by clicking on the drop-down under the role.
7. You can designate one contact as the primary contact by clicking the radio button in the primary column next to that contact's name.
8. When you have added all the contacts, click Save.

Your company's Salesforce administrator can set up the list of contact roles in the Setup area of Salesforce. You can identify as many roles as you need.

Once you have developed a good rapport with your primary contact in the opportunity, you should ask about any other individuals who might play a role in the decision-making process, and then add those contacts and their roles to the opportunity in Salesforce.

To view opportunities, you'll need **Read** permission on **Opportunities**.

To edit opportunities, you'll need **Edit** permission on **Opportunities**.

Contact Roles for Huge Deal

Primary	Contact	Role
○	No Primary Contact	
◉	Rachel Ciupek-Reed	Decision Maker
○	Jane Keene	Executive Sponsor
○	Stacy Roach	Influencer
○		—None—
○		—None—
○		—None—

This feature is available in:

✔ Unlimited ✔ Developer
✔ Enterprise ✔ Group
✔ Professional ✔ Personal

Task E   Creating an opportunity when converting a lead

A lead is a potential opportunity, and in Salesforce when you convert a lead, the application lets you create an opportunity so that you can begin tracking that potential deal through your sales cycle.

To create an opportunity from a lead:

1. Click in the Leads tab to go to the Leads home view.
2. Find the lead you want to convert and click on the name of the person or company of the lead.
3. Click the Convert button.
4. In the Convert Lead section, add or change any information and click Convert.
5. You will now be in the Account view; to edit the opportunity created when you converted the lead, click on the opportunity name in the Opportunities section.
6. You can now add products, or edit the information in the Opportunity Detail section.

If you don't want to create an opportunity when you convert a lead, simply check the box labeled Do not create a new opportunity upon conversion.

To convert leads, you'll need **Create** and **Edit** permissions on **Leads**, **Accounts**, **Contacts**, and **Opportunities**, as well as **Convert Leads** and **Read** on any related campaigns.

To edit opportunities and opportunity products, you'll need **Edit** permission on **Opportunities**.

This feature is available in:

✔ Unlimited	✔ Developer
✔ Enterprise	✔ Group
✔ Professional	Personal

Task F   Cloning an opportunity

If you have an opportunity that is similar to an existing opportunity, you can
save yourself time and typing by cloning that opportunity. This can be a big
time saver, particularly if the opportunity includes a lot of products.

To clone an opportunity:

1. Click on the Opportunities tab and filter the view to find the opportunity
   you would like to clone.
2. Select the opportunity by clicking on the opportunity name.
3. In the Opportunity Detail section, click the Clone button.
4. Add or change any of the information in the Opportunity Edit screen and
   click Save.
5. You will now be viewing the new opportunity that you created using the
   cloning option.

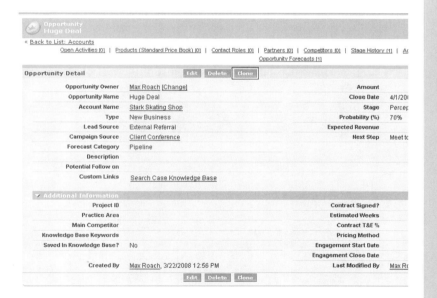

If you are cloning an opportunity
owned by another user, when you are
in the Opportunity Edit screen, you
will not be able to change the
Opportunity Owner to yourself, but
when you save the new opportunity,
you will be the opportunity owner. If
you have the correct user privileges,
you can then change the opportunity
owner to another user.

When you clone an opportunity, if
your company requires products on
opportunities, you will only see the
Clone button. If your company does
not require products on opportunities
then clicking the Clone button will
produce a drop-down menu, with the
option to Clone with products, or
Clone without products.

To clone opportunities, you'll
need **Create** permission on
Opportunities.

To view opportunity products,
you'll need **Read** permission on
Opportunities, **Products**, and
Price Books.

To edit opportunity products,
you'll need **Edit** permission on
Opportunities.

This feature is available in:

✔ Unlimited   ✔ Developer
✔ Enterprise   ✔ Group
✔ Professional   ✔ Personal

Task G   Editing opportunities

As an opportunity moves through the sales cycle, you will need to update or edit the opportunity to reflect the new stages. Also, the details of the opportunity may change over time, so you will need to edit the opportunity to reflect the new information. Inline editing is also available for changing information for an opportunity.

To edit an opportunity:

1. Click on the Opportunities tab and filter the view to find the opportunity you would like to edit.
2. Select the opportunity by clicking on the opportunity name.
3. To edit the information in the Opportunity Detail section, click Edit. You can then change the expected close date or the stage. If your organization has enabled customizable forecasting, you can also select the forecast category.
4. To add products to the Products section, click Add Product. If you want to edit the existing products associated with the opportunity, click Edit All. You can then change the quantity, sales price, or line description.
5. Changes made to the Opportunity Amount, Stage, Probability, and Close Date will update the Stage History section at the bottom of the opportunity view.

It is important to keep the data in your opportunities current, as this is the data that will be pulled into any sales reports and forecasts.

🔒 To edit opportunities, you'll need **Edit** permission on **Opportunities**.

🔒 To view opportunity products, you'll need **Read** permission on **Opportunities**, **Products**, and **Price Books**.

🔒 To edit opportunity products, you'll need **Edit** permission on **Opportunities**.

This feature is available in:

✔ Unlimited   ✔ Developer

✔ Enterprise   ✔ Group

✔ Professional   ✔ Personal

Task H   Closing opportunities

As you closely work a deal, shepherding it through the sales process, at some point all your diligence and hard work will be rewarded when you win the opportunity! Or, unthinkable as it is, you may lose the opportunity. Either way, you need to update the Stage in the opportunity so that your sales reports and forecasts will accurately reflect the opportunities you won, as well as those you lost.

To close an opportunity:

1. Click on the Opportunities tab and filter the view to find the opportunity you would like to close.
2. Select the opportunity you want to close by clicking on the opportunity name.
3. Click Edit in the Opportunity Detail section.
4. Change the Stage to Closed Won or Closed Lost and click Save.

Analyzing both your wins and losses will help you to improve over time and hopefully lead to a greater percentage of deals won. In addition, looking at the reasons why you win or lose deals can help identify trends in your industry, rising competitors, as well as internal, organization obstacles to closing more deals.

To close opportunities, you'll need **Edit** permission on **Opportunities**.

This feature is available in:

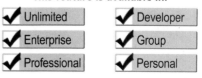

✔ Unlimited   ✔ Developer
✔ Enterprise   ✔ Group
✔ Professional ✔ Personal

Task I Deleting opportunities

If an opportunity is no longer valid, and you didn't win or lose the deal, you might want to delete it. You can remove an opportunity from Salesforce easily, right from an Opportunity list view. Just be aware that deleting an opportunity also deletes all the associated information on that opportunity.

To delete an opportunity:

1. Click on the Opportunities tab and filter the view to find the opportunity you would like to delete.
2. Click Del next to the opportunity name in the Opportunity list view.
3. You will be prompted to confirm the deletion, click OK.
4. The opportunity will be deleted.

When you delete an opportunity, all of the associated items, such as Open Activities, Activity History, Notes & Attachments, Contact Roles, Partners, Competitors, and all the Stage History are also deleted. If the opportunity was lost, you don't want to delete it, because analyzing the deals you lose can help provide insight so that you can improve your close rate on future opportunities.

If you inadvertently delete an opportunity, you can retrieve that opportunity from the Recycle Bin. Simply click on the Recycle Bin in the left sidebar, and click the check box next to the opportunity you want to recover and click Undelete. This will restore the opportunity, and all the other associated details, to your opportunity list.

To delete opportunities, you'll need **Delete** permission on **Opportunities**.

This feature is available in:

✓ Unlimited	✓ Developer
✓ Enterprise	✓ Group
✓ Professional	✓ Personal

Task J   Sharing opportunities

If you work in a team selling environment, you may need to share your opportunities with other users in your organization. This is only necessary if your Salesforce administrator did not set up a public sharing model. You can allow colleagues to view your opportunities when you share.

To share opportunities:

1. Click on the Opportunities tab and filter the view to find the opportunity you would like to share.
2. Select the opportunity you want to share by clicking on the opportunity name.
3. Click the Sharing button in the Opportunity Detail view.
4. To view the current access list for this opportunity, click the Expand List button; this will show all the users that have access to that opportunity based on their existing user level within Salesforce. To understand why a particular user is already on the Share list, click the Why link to the left of the user's name.
5. To add a user, click the Add button.
6. In the New Sharing screen, choose the area to search from in the dropdown and search by public groups, roles, roles and subordinates, and users. You can either search for a specific group, role, or user, or select a user from the list on the left under Currently Not Shared and click the right-facing arrow to move that user to the New Sharing list on the right.
7. Setting the user's access to the opportunity is required; click in the dropdown and select Read Only, which will allow that user to view the opportunity, but not edit it; or select Read/Write, which will allow that user to both view and edit the opportunity.
8. Click Save.

If your organization has set the security control for all opportunities to Public Read/Write, then you won't see the Sharing button on the opportunity. But if the sharing settings for opportunities have been set to Private or Public Read Only, then you will see the Sharing button.

You can simplify sharing by setting the sharing option on the Account level, so that everything associated with that account, including opportunities, will be set. The other option would be to set up Team Selling. For more information on the team selling feature of Salesforce, click on the Help link at the top of the Salesforce screen and search for "team selling" (without quotes).

To share opportunities, you'll need **Edit** permission on **Opportunities**.

You also need to be the owner of the opportunity, or you must be above the owner in the hierarchy.

This feature is available in:

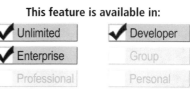

✔ Unlimited   ✔ Developer

✔ Enterprise   Group

Professional   Personal

Viewing and monitoring opportunities

Once you have entered your opportunities into Salesforce, you have several options for viewing those opportunities. You can also track additional information about the deals in your pipeline, such as detailed information on your competition in an opportunity. You can even set alerts to email you and other folks in your organization when an opportunity crosses a particular revenue and probability threshold.

Task A   Viewing the opportunity list

There are several predefined viewing options when you want to see a list of your opportunities. These include viewing just your own opportunities, all the deals closing this month or next month, the new opportunities this week or last week, and the opportunities that were wins. You can even customize your own list view, so that you are looking at just the opportunities you need to track.

To view the opportunity list:

1. Click on the Opportunities tab to go to the Opportunities home view.
2. Click on the View pull-down to select from a predefined list of opportunity views, such as All Opportunities, Closing Next Month, Closing This Month, My Opportunities, New Last Week, New This Week, Private, Recently Viewed Opportunities, and Won.
3. You can sort the opportunity list by clicking on the column headers at the top of the list.
4. You can print the list by clicking the Printable View link in the top-right corner of the list, next to the Help for this Page link.
5. You can also create a custom view by clicking on the Create New View link next to the drop-down of predefined views. For more information on customizing list views, see Chapter 5.

For detailed instructions on customizing your own list views, see Chapter 5 of this book.

Once you have the list view of your opportunities that you want, you can sort that list by clicking on any of the column headers. Once you have the list sorted by the column you like, such as Account Name, you can create a quick view by clicking on a letter in the alphabet in the list view, and that will bring up all the opportunities for accounts that start with that letter.

To view opportunities, you'll need **Read** permission on **Opportunities**.

This feature is available in:

✔ Unlimited   ✔ Developer
✔ Enterprise   ✔ Group
✔ Professional   ✔ Personal

Task B   Finding opportunities

Mastering the search functionality is pretty critical in any sales tool, and Salesforce is no different. If you diligently enter all of your opportunities, then being able to quickly find a specific opportunity when you need to update it is important. Luckily, the searching capabilities of Salesforce make it easy.

To find an opportunity:

1. Click on the Search All drop-down menu in the Search area in the left sidebar and select Opportunities.
2. In the search box, enter the information you want to search on, such as the opportunity name or the account name. Select the Limit to items I own check box to have the search only return your opportunities.
3. After searching by either the simple sidebar search or advanced search, all the results are returned in a list view that can be sorted by the column headers.
4. To select an opportunity, simply click on the opportunity name. Clicking on the account name will take you to the account view.

When you are using the Advanced Search function, if you are searching on a word or phrase that appears in an item associated with an opportunity, like a note, activity, or history, then you will need to also click the check box next to those entities in the Advanced Search Scope section in order to find that information.

While working with searches related to opportunities, I was not able to search by a product name, or part of a product name, nor could I search for opportunities by the opportunity owner. You can create a new view and filter by opportunity owner, however.

To view opportunities, you'll need **Read** permission on **Opportunities**.

This feature is available in:

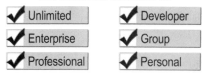

✔ Unlimited ✔ Developer
✔ Enterprise ✔ Group
✔ Professional ✔ Personal

Task C   Setting alerts for big deals

All opportunities are important, but sometimes there is a lot of noise to sift through to keep tabs on the large, important deals. Salesforce allows you to create a Big Deal Alert. (That is actually what it's called in the application!) You can set a threshold by amount and probability, which will automatically email all the folks in your organization that need to be aware of those big deals.

To activate an alert for a big deal:

1. Click the Setup | App Setup | Customize | Opportunities | Big Deal Alert link on the top-right area of the Salesforce screen.

2. Click Customize | Opportunities | Big Deal Alert in the App Setup area on the left sidebar.

3. Give the alert a name, such as "Big Deal" in Step 1. Alert Name.

4. In Step 2 Threshold, enter the Trigger Amount and Trigger Probability. The alert will only activate for those opportunities that meet the minimum for both the amount and probability you entered.

5. In Step 3 Alert Settings, click the check box to make the alert Active, and fill in the email name and address that the alert will come from when it is sent.

6. In Step 4 Recipients, add all the Notify, Notify CC, and Notify BCC emails for everyone you want to receive the alert, separating each email address by a comma. Check the Notify Opportunity Owner to also send an alert to the owner.

7. Click Save.

A couple of things to note about alerts—first, an opportunity will trigger an alert the first time it crosses the combined threshold you set for the opportunity amount and probability, but it will not send subsequent alerts if either of those increase. So if the deal gets bigger or the probability increases, you won't get additional alerts for that deal. If, however, the deal drops below the minimum thresholds, and then later crosses the threshold amounts, a new alert will be generated at the time that the opportunity again reaches the minimum amounts to trigger the alert.

To activate the Big Deal Alert, you'll need **Customize Application** permission.

This feature is available in:

✔ Unlimited	✔ Developer
✔ Enterprise	✔ Group
✔ Professional	Personal

Task D Tracking your competition

Smart sales people follow the old adage, "Keep your friends close, but keep your enemies closer." Maybe it's a stretch to think of your competitors as enemies, because after all, competition validates your "space," right? Whatever your view of your competitors, understanding who you are up against in a potential deal, and what their strengths and weaknesses are, can only help you in that opportunity.

To define your primary competitors:

1. Click Setup | App Setup | Customize | Opportunities | Competitors.
2. Click the New button and add each competitor on its own line.
3. Click Save.

> **Add Picklist Values**
> **Competitors**
>
> Add one or more picklist values below. Each value should be on its own line.
>
> Evil Competitor, LLC
> ABC Company
> Sortofa Competitor, Inc.
> Competition Major, Ltd
>
> Save   Cancel

It is important to maintain your list of competitors, because in most industries, that list can grow, shrink, and change over time. Having the list up-to-date makes it easier for busy sales representatives to track competitors in an opportunity. This task is usually done by your Salesforce administrator.

🔒 To define competitors, you'll need **Customize Application** permission.

This feature is available in:

✔ Unlimited   ✔ Developer
✔ Enterprise   ✔ Group
✔ Professional   ✔ Personal

There are two places to enter information about your competitors. In the Opportunity Detail view, there is a field for Main Competitor(s). And, in the Competitors section, you add competitors from your defined list of competitors, with the added bonus of being able to enter their specific strengths and weaknesses, as they pertain to this opportunity.

To edit opportunities, you'll need **Edit** permission on **Opportunities**.

Task E   Adding competitive information to an opportunity

Being realistic about your competition in an opportunity is vital to understanding that opportunity. Who your biggest competitors are may shift from deal to deal, or industry to industry. Someone who is a real threat in one deal, might be relatively inconsequential in a deal that doesn't play to their strengths. Salesforce lets you add detailed information about your competitor's strengths and weaknesses on a deal-by-deal basis.

To add competitive information to an opportunity:

1. Click on the Opportunities tab and filter the view to find the opportunity you would like to close.
2. Select the opportunity you want to add competitive information to by clicking on the opportunity name.
3. Scroll down to the Competitors section and click New.
4. If your company has defined a list of competitors, you can click the Competitor Name Combo icon to the right of the Competitor Name field and select the competitor.
5. In the Strengths section list the competitor's strengths, with each item on its own line.
6. In the Weaknesses section list the competitor's weaknesses, with each item on its own line.
7. Click Save and repeat steps 3-6 for each company you are competing against in this opportunity.

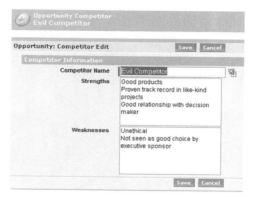

This feature is available in:

Task F   Viewing opportunity customization options and settings

Customizing your opportunities is an easy way to extend the power of Salesforce. Customization allows you to track information about an opportunity that is specific to your sales cycle or business model.

To view the opportunity customization options and settings:

1. Click Setup | App Setup | Customize | Opportunities.
2. Select the area you want to view, such as fields.
3. You will be able to view the list of fields used in opportunities, with the specific information like Data Type displayed.
4. To view detailed information on a field, including the definition, click the field name.
5. Once in the detail view of a specific opportunity field, click the View Field Accessibility button and the user profiles with their associated Field Access will be displayed.
6. For more information about any of the areas you select, simply click the Help icon in the top-right corner of each screen.

The following items can be customized for opportunities:

- Fields
- Validation Rules
- Triggers
- Contact Roles
- Competitors
- Page Layouts
- Search Layouts
- Buttons and Links
- Sales Processes
- Record Types
- Settings
- Opportunity Products

The fields in the opportunity are different depending on which Salesforce edition you are using. And field level security, the ability to control which users can view and/or edit particular fields, is only available in the Unlimited, Enterprise, and Developer Editions.

To customize opportunity items, you'll need **Customize Application** permission.

Field
Stage   Help for this Page

Back to Opportunity Fields

View Field Accessibility

Field Label   Stage   Field Name   StageName
Data Type   Picklist

Below is a list of dependent fields whose values are filtered based on the values in this picklist.

No dependencies defined.

Validation Rules   Validation Rules Help

No validation rules defined.

Below is the master list of picklist values for the Opportunity Stages field.

Click Edit to change the picklist value. Click New to add a value to the picklist. Click Reorder to change the sequence of values in the list.

Opportunity Stages Picklist Values   Printable View   Opportunity Stages Picklist Values Help

Stage Name	Type	Probability	Forecast Category	Modified By
Prospecting	Open	10%	Pipeline	Carol Gilliland, 1/9/2008 3:12 PM
Qualification	Open	10%	Pipeline	Carol Gilliland, 1/9/2008 3:12 PM
Needs Analysis	Open	20%	Pipeline	Carol Gilliland, 1/9/2008 3:12 PM
Value Proposition	Open	50%	Pipeline	Carol Gilliland, 1/9/2008 3:12 PM
Id. Decision Makers	Open	60%	Pipeline	Carol Gilliland, 1/9/2008 3:12 PM
Perception Analysis	Open	70%	Pipeline	Carol Gilliland, 1/9/2008 3:12 PM
Proposal/Price Quote	Open	75%	Pipeline	Carol Gilliland, 1/9/2008 3:12 PM
Negotiation/Review	Open	90%	Pipeline	Carol Gilliland, 1/9/2008 3:12 PM
Closed Won	Closed/Won	100%	Closed	Carol Gilliland, 1/9/2008 3:12 PM
Closed Lost	Closed/Lost	0%	Omitted	Carol Gilliland, 1/9/2008 3:12 PM

Inactive Values Picklist Values

No Inactive Values values defined.

This feature is available in:

✔ Unlimited   ✔ Developer
✔ Enterprise   ✔ Group
✔ Professional   ✔ Personal

Managing products

Products are what you sell, and can include both traditional products, like widgets, as well as services. Carefully managing your products in Salesforce will make your sales reports and forecasts more meaningful. You can even set up schedules for your products, so that you can more effectively track and manage delivery of products and revenue over time.

Task A   Viewing products

From the Products home tab, you can view all products, as well as products you recently viewed or edited. You can even customize your own list view, so that you are looking at just the products you typically need.

To view products:

1. Click on the Products tab to go to the Products home.
2. To view price books, select the price book from the View drop-down in the price book section.
3. To view products, click All Products from the View drop-down in the Product Views section.
4. To view assets, click All Assets from the View drop-down in the Asset Views section.
5. Recent products that you have viewed or have added to opportunities will be listed in the Recent Products section.
6. In the Reports section, there is a short-cut to Reports.
7. In the Maintenance section, you can select Manage Price Books or Mass Delete Products.

For detailed instructions on customizing your own list views, see Chapter 5 of this book.

Once you have the list view of your products that you want, you can sort that list by clicking on any of the column headers, such as Product Name or Product Family.

To view products, you'll need **Read** permission on **Products**.

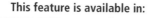

This feature is available in:

✔ Unlimited   ✔ Developer

✔ Enterprise   Group

$ Professional   Personal

Task B   Finding products

If there is one skill that will help you when navigating your sales tool, it's the skill of the hunt. Searching for specific data—the easier and faster you can find what you need, the more productive you will be. If your organization only has a big, long list of products and services, then being able to quickly find a specific product when you need it is vitally important. Luckily, the searching capabilities of Salesforce make it easy.

To find products:

1. Click on the Products tab to go to the Products home page.
2. In the search box, enter the product you are searching for. You can enter part of the product name with a wildcard operator.
3. Once you have started a search on the Products home tab, you can then choose to search by keyword or by using field filters. If you search by both, then the results will have to meet both the data you entered in the keyword text box, as well as the criteria you filtered on in the field filters.
4. You can use field filters to find part of a product name. In the Filter Field drop-down, choose the Product Name option.
5. Your search results are returned in a list view, where you can then select the product.

The search in the left sidebar does not allow for finding products and price books and neither does the Advanced Search. To find a product, you can search from the Products home tab, or when you are adding products to an opportunity.

To view Price Books, you'll need **Read** permission on **Products** and **Price Books**.

To view Products, you'll need **Read** permission on **Products**.

Product Search — Help for this Page

Enter your keyword and filter criteria, then click Search to begin your search. Click More filters to use more than one filter. Search results include all records that match both your keyword and filter entries.

Find Products [10]   My Columns

By Keyword	By Field Filter			
gen*	--None--	--None--		More filters >>

Search

Keyword: "gen*"

Action	Product Name	Product Code	Product Description	Product Family
Edit | Deactivate	GenWatt Diesel 1200kW	GWD1200	The 1200 kilowatt GenWatt Diesel Generator	
Edit | Deactivate	GenWatt Gasoline 2000kW	GC5060		
Edit | Deactivate	GenWatt Gasoline 300kW	GC5020		
Edit | Deactivate	GenWatt Gasoline 750kW	GC5040		
Edit | Deactivate	GenWatt Diesel 1000kW	GC1060		
Edit | Deactivate	GenWatt Propane 1500kW	GC3060		
Edit | Deactivate	GenWatt Propane 100kW	GC3020		
Edit | Deactivate	GenWatt Propane 500kW	GC3040		
Edit | Deactivate	GenWatt Diesel 10kW	GC1020		
Edit | Deactivate	GenWatt Diesel 200kW	GC1040		

This feature is available in:

✔ Unlimited   ✔ Developer
✔ Enterprise   Group
$ Professional   Personal

Task C   Creating a product

It's exciting to be able to offer your customers a new product or service. Adding that product or service to the Products home tab in Salesforce is easy and painless.

Price books are a way to organize products. If you add a new product, it will automatically be added to a standard price book as well as any custom price books that you add that product to, making the standard price book a master list of all products and prices.

To view products, you'll need **Read** permission on **Products**.

To create products, you'll need **Create** permission on **Products**.

To create a product:

1. Click in the Products tab to go to the Products home view.
2. Click on the Create New button in the left sidebar and choose Product.
3. Enter the Product Name, Product Code if there is one, and a Product Description.
4. Click the check box to make this new product active.
5. If you want to enter a standard price for the product, click Save & Add Price, otherwise, just click Save.
6. If you selected Save & Add Price, you can enter the standard price and then click Save.
7. To add the new product to an existing price book, click the Add to Price Book button in the price books section of the product view and click the check box in front of the price book you want to add the new product to, or select the standard price book and click Select. You will then be prompted to enter a list price for the product in the price book. Then click Save.

This feature is available in:

✔ Unlimited   ✔ Developer

✔ Enterprise   Group

$ Professional   Personal

Task D Cloning products

If you have a new product or service that is similar to an existing product, you can save yourself time and typing by cloning that product. This is particularly helpful if you set default schedules for your products, as you can keep the default schedules the same for similar products.

To clone a product:

1. Click on the Products tab and click on the All Products drop-down in the Product Views section. Find the product you would like to clone.
2. Select the product by clicking on the product name.
3. In the Product Detail section, click the Clone button.
4. Enter the new Product Name and click Save.
5. In the Standard Price section, click the Edit link to change the Standard Price, enter the new product name and click Save.
6. You will now be viewing the new product that you created using the cloning option.

If you use specific product codes, be careful when cloning products, as the product code is also cloned, creating two products with the same code.

To view products, you'll need **Read** permission on **Products**.

To clone products, you'll need **Create** permission on **Products** and **View** permission on **Price Books**.

Product
Sales Process Review

‹ Back to List: Accounts

Printable View | Customize Page | Help for this Page

Standard Price [1] | Price Books [0]

Product Detail [Edit] [Delete] [Clone]

Product Name	Sales Process Review	Product Family	
Product Code	Serv_SPR	Active	✓
Product Description			
Created By	Max Roach, 3/22/2008 1:01 PM	Last Modified By	Max Roach, 3/22/2008 1:01 PM

[Edit] [Delete] [Clone]

Standard Price   Standard Price Help

Action		Standard Price	Active
Edit	Del	$25,000.00	✓

Price Books   [Add to Price Book]   Price Books Help

No records to display

∧ Back To Top   Always show me ▼ more records per related list

This feature is available in:

✔ Unlimited   ✔ Developer
✔ Enterprise   Group
$ Professional   Personal

Task E   Editing products

Managing your products well means keeping your products up-to-date. Invalid or incorrect information on a product could well result in a quote going to a prospect or customer with incorrect information. Some information is not as critical, but price would be an important element to keep current on your products.

To view products, you'll need **Read** permission on **Products**.

To edit products, you'll need **Edit** permission on **Products**.

To edit a product:

1. Click on the Products tab and click on the All Products drop-down in the Product Views section. Find the product you would like to edit.
2. Select the product by clicking on the product name.
3. In the Product Detail section, click the Edit button.
4. Edit the Product Name, Product Code, and Product Description and click Save.
5. To edit the price of a product, click the Edit link next to the Standard Price in the Standard Price section, update the price, and click Save.
6. To add the product to another price book, click the Add to Price Book button.

This feature is available in:

✔ Unlimited	✔ Developer
✔ Enterprise	Group
$ Professional	Personal

Task F   Deleting products

You may want to delete or remove a product that you no longer offer. You first need to make sure that it's not currently listed on any open opportunities, and if it is, you will need to remove it from all of those opportunities before deleting. You might consider editing the product and clearing the Active check box, thus deactivating the product, rather than deleting it.

To delete a product:

1. Click on the Products tab and click on the All Products drop-down in the Product Views section. Find the product you would like to delete.
2. Select the product by clicking on the product name.
3. In the Product Detail section, click the Delete button.
4. You will be prompted to confirm the deletion; click OK.
5. The product will be deleted.

If you inadvertently delete a product, you can retrieve that product from the Recycle Bin. Simply click on the Recycle Bin in the left sidebar, and click the check box next to the product you want to recover and click Undelete. This will restore the product.

If you try to delete a product that is on an existing opportunity, Salesforce will display a list of the opportunities that use that product. You will need to remove the product from each opportunity before you can delete it. If you don't want to remove the product from the opportunities, just deactivate the product.

To delete products, you'll need **Delete** permission on **Products**.

This feature is available in:

63

The administrator for your organization will have to enable scheduling in the application setup first.

You can also edit a product from the Products home tab and set a default schedule.

To create schedules, you'll need **Edit** permission on **Opportunities**.

Task G Creating schedules from an opportunity

For many organizations, just tracking an opportunity, with its associated product(s) and revenue, is sufficient. For other organizations, understanding how those products and revenue will be distributed over time is important. The close date is just the start of the product and revenue flow, and properly forecasting that flow is important.

To create a schedule from an opportunity:

1. Click on the Opportunities tab to go to the Opportunities home page.
2. Find the opportunity that you want to create a schedule for and click on the opportunity name.
3. In the Product(s) section, click the product name.
4. In the Schedule section, click Establish.
5. In the Type drop-down, select if the schedule will be Quantity, Revenue, or both.
6. In the Establish Quantity Schedule section, enter the Start Date for the schedule and the Quantity. For Schedule Type you can either select Divide Amount into multiple installments or Repeat Amount for each installment.
7. In the Installment Period drop-down, select the frequency of the schedule: Daily, Weekly, Monthly, Quarterly, or Yearly.
8. Enter the Number of Installments for the schedule. Repeat for the Revenue Schedule if applicable and click Save. You will be viewing the quantity and/or revenue schedule you created. Click Save again to return to the Opportunity Product Detail view.

This feature is available in:

✔ Unlimited   ✔ Developer
✔ Enterprise   Group
$ Professional Personal

Managing price books

Price books are basically collections of products with their standard prices. You might want to organize your products and services into discreet price books, which can make it easier to add products to opportunities, as you can select the appropriate price book and then you are only viewing the products within that price book.

Task A Creating a price book

Creating a price book is a straightforward task, and all the information on price books is located on the Products home tab. Once you have created your new price book, see the next task, Task B: Adding products to a price book.

To create a price book:

1. Click on the Products tab to go to the Products home page.
2. In the Maintenance section, below the list of Recent Products, click Manage Price Books.
3. In the Active Price Books section, click New.
4. Enter the name for the new price book, which is a required field, and a description.
5. Click the Active check box to make this new price book active.
6. You can clone the contents of an existing price book by selecting the price book from the Existing Price Books drop-down.
7. Click Save.

You might want to take a step back and a big breath and really think through the organization of your price books and products. Like most cool features of any customer relationship management tool, it's only as good as your input to it— meaning, that you can quickly create a little mess if you don't do some good planning up front.

To view Price Books, you'll need **Read** permission on **Products** and **Price Books**.

To create Price Books, you'll need **Create** permission on **Price Books**.

This feature is available in:

✔ Unlimited	✔ Developer
✔ Enterprise	Group
$ Professional	Personal

Task B   Adding products to a price book

Once you have created your price books, you can add products to them and set the List Price for each of the products and services that are in your new price book.

To add products to a price book:

1. Click on the Products tab to go to the Products home page.
2. In the Maintenance section, below the list of Recent Products, click Manage Price Books.
3. Click on the name of the price book to which you want to add products.
4. In the Products section, click Add.
5. Click the check box next to each of the products you want to add to the price book and click Select.
6. Adjust the List Price, or click the check box to use the Standard Price as the List Price.
7. Click Save.

If you have a lot of products to add, and you are going to use the Standard Price, you can check the box next to each of the product names, and then when you click Select and Save you will have added a whole crop of products all at once.

To edit Price Books, you'll need **Edit** permission on **Products** and **Price Books**.

This feature is available in:

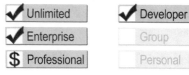

✔ Unlimited   ✔ Developer
✔ Enterprise   Group
$ Professional   Personal

Task C   Cloning price books

If you have a category of products and services that is similar to an existing price book, you can save yourself time and typing by cloning that price book.

To clone a price book:

1. Click on the Products tab to go to the Products home page.
2. In the Maintenance section, below the list of Recent Products, click Manage Price Books.
3. In the Active Price Books section, click on the name of the price book you want to clone and click Clone.
4. Enter the name for the new price book, which is a required field, and a description.
5. Click the Active check box to make this new price book active and click Save.

Cloning a price book includes the products, so you will be starting this new price book with an existing set of products and services.

To view Price Books, you'll need **Read** permission on **Products** and **Price Books**.

To clone Price Books, you'll need **Create** permission on **Price Books**.

This feature is available in:

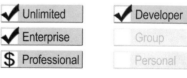

Managing your sales forecast

Accurate forecasting may well be the Holy Grail of sales. Everyone, sales representatives included, wants an accurate forecast. Wikipedia defines forecasting as "The process of estimation in unknown situations." A perusal of Webster's definitions includes terms like "predict," "conjecture," "plan," and, my personal favorite, "guess." Sometimes forecasting can seem like guessing, but accurately forecasting the sale of specific products and services, and the associated revenue, is critical to most businesses' planning.

Task A   Setting up customizable forecasting

Salesforce offers two forecasting models: the standard model and a customizable forecast. This section is only concerned with the customizable forecast, because the ability to customize your forecast is pretty critical to accurate forecasting. With customizable forecasting, you can configure forecasting in Salesforce to more closely match your organization's sales and forecasting cycles.

To set up customizable forecasting:

1. Click Setup | Customize | Forecasts | Forecast Hierarchy.
2. Click the Enable Customizable Forecasting button and click OK.
3. To add the opportunity forecast list and forecast category field to your opportunity page layouts, click the check box next to the layout. Click the check box for Append to users' personal related list customization to allow other users to add forecast data to their custom list views. Click Save.
4. Click on Settings and in the Forecast Data Aggregation section, click the check boxes to Forecast Revenue or Forecast Quantity, or both. Set your Forecast Period to Monthly or Quarterly. Set the Forecast Date to the Opportunity Close Date or the Product Date. In Forecast Type set to Use Overall Forecast or Use Product Families.
5. In the Forecast Summary Default View, select Product Family, if enabled, and the Default Start Range and Duration and the Forecast Numbers, if you selected both Revenue and Quantity.
6. In the Forecast Data Sharing section, click the check box to Enable Forecast Sharing if you want to allow administrators and managers to share forecasts with other users.
7. Click Save.

You can also set up a forecast hierarchy, so that if you are a manager with sales representatives reporting to you, you can view a roll-up of your group's forecast.

For tips on setting up customizable forecasting, there is a great cheat sheet in the Help & Support section of Salesforce.

To set up Customizable Forecasting, you'll need to be a Salesforce Administrator.

This feature is available in:

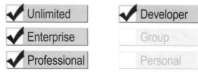

✔ Unlimited	✔ Developer
✔ Enterprise	Group
✔ Professional	Personal

Task B   Viewing your forecast

Clicking on the Forecasts tab will allow you to view, update, and submit your forecast. When you go to the Forecasts home tab, by default you are viewing just your own forecast. If you have the proper permission, you can click the lookup icon next to your name and select another user's forecast, such as a user that reports to you.

To view your forecast:

1. Click on the Forecasts tab to go to the Forecasts home page.
2. You will be viewing your current forecast. You can click on the Forecast History button to see the forecasts you have submitted. Click the Back to Forecast link at the top of the Forecast History view to return to the Forecast view.
3. You can make changes to the Forecast Numbers, choosing either Revenue or Quantity. You can change the start date of the forecast, as well as the length. In the Display Units drop-down, you can select Exact Value, Whole Numbers, Thousands, Millions, or % Quota.
4. You can view the opportunities that make up your forecast numbers by clicking the Opportunities tab.

There are four forecast categories in Salesforce: Pipeline, Best Case, Commit, and Closed. These categories are populated by the stage of the opportunities that make up your forecast. Your administrator can map the forecast category to an opportunity stage. For example, the Commit category may be mapped to the Closed Won stage, but that can be changed in the Setup.

If you are a manager with other users reporting to you, you will see the roll-up of their forecasts.

To view opportunity products, you'll need **Read** permission on **Opportunities**, **Products**, and **Price Books**.

Teddy Dawg's Forecast				Printable View | Help for this Page

Teddy Dawg's Forecast: Find a Forecast:
Sales Representative   [By User ▼] [Dawg Teddy] 🔍

Max Roach » Richard Roach » Edward Roach »
Felix Dawg (Sales Representative) | Teddy Dawg (Sales Representative)

[Forecast History]

Forecast Numbers:	Range Start:		Range Length:	Display Units:
[Revenue and Quantity ▼]	[March ▼]	[FY 2008 ▼]	[3 periods ▼]	[Exact Value ▼]

Forecast Category	March FY 2008	April FY 2008	May FY 2008	Totals
Quota	$0.00 / 0.00	$0.00 / 0.00	$0.00 / 0.00	$0.00 / 0.00
Closed	$0.00 / 0.00	$0.00 / 0.00	$0.00 / 0.00	$0.00 / 0.00
Commit	$0.00 / 0.00	$0.00 / 0.00	$0.00 / 0.00	$0.00 / 0.00
Best Case	$0.00 / 0.00	$0.00 / 0.00	$0.00 / 0.00	$0.00 / 0.00
Pipeline	$35,000.00 / 0.00	$12,000.00 / 0.00	$0.00 / 0.00	$47,000.00 / 0.00

Forecasts	Opportunities

Teddy Dawg

Forecast Period	Closed	Commit	Best Case	Pipeline
March FY 2008	$0.00 / 0.00	$0.00 / 0.00	$0.00 / 0.00	$35,000.00 / 0.00
April FY 2008	$0.00 / 0.00	$0.00 / 0.00	$0.00 / 0.00	$12,000.00 / 0.00
May FY 2008	$0.00 / 0.00	$0.00 / 0.00	$0.00 / 0.00	$0.00 / 0.00

This feature is available in:

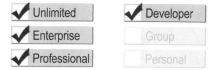

✔ Unlimited	✔ Developer
✔ Enterprise	Group
✔ Professional	Personal

Task C   Updating your forecast

Prior to submitting your forecast, you may want to update your forecast. The first place to start is the opportunities that make up your forecast. Once you have updated your opportunities, those are reflected in your forecast.

To update your forecast:

1. You need to update the opportunities that make up your forecast in order to update your forecast. Click on the Forecasts tab to go to the Forecasts home page. Click on the Opportunities tab.

2. Select the opportunity by clicking on the opportunity name.

3. To edit the information in the Opportunity Detail section, click Edit. You can then change the expected Close Date or the Stage. You can also update the Forecast Category, so that even if the stage of the opportunity does not map to the forecast category, you can manually change it here.

4. To add products to the Products section, click Add product. If you want to edit the existing products associated with the opportunity, click Edit All. You can then change the quantity, sales price, or line description.

5. Changes made to the opportunity amount, stage, probability, close date, and forecast category will update your forecast.

You can also update your forecast by editing opportunities in the Opportunities home tab.

To edit opportunities, you'll need **Edit** permission on **Opportunities**.

To view opportunity products, you'll need **Read** permission on **Opportunities**, **Products**, and **Price Books**.

To edit opportunity products, you'll need **Edit** permission on **Opportunities**.

This feature is available in:

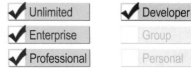

✔ Unlimited   ✔ Developer
✔ Enterprise   Group
✔ Professional   Personal

Task D Overriding your forecast

The amounts in your forecast categories of Closed, Commit, Best Case, and Pipeline are determined by the opportunity stage of each deal in your forecast. You might have some opportunities that you either want to include or exclude in one of those categories, even if the opportunity stage is not technically mapped to one of those forecast categories. You can edit the opportunity and adjust the forecast category to override the standard mapping setup by your Salesforce Administrator. This is a task that is only done by managers or administrators.

To override your forecast:

1. Click on the Forecasts tab to go to the Forecasts home page. Click on the Opportunities tab in the Forecast home view.
2. Click the Edit link next to the opportunity you want to override.
3. In the Opportunity Forecast Edit section, update the Stage, Forecast Category, and Close Date. You can also add any Forecast Comments.
4. In the Products section, if you have more than one product associated with an opportunity, click the check box for Change Category and select the appropriate Product Forecast Category from the drop-down.
5. Click Save. Click on the Forecasts tab. You will now see an icon next to the amount under the category indicating that you overrode the forecast.

In addition to overriding the forecast stage, you can adjust the overall forecast amount as well. In your Forecast view, click the pencil icon next to the amount you want to adjust in any of your forecast categories and override the amount by entering a new amount.

If you are a sales manager, with direct reports, you can choose to accept, reject, or override the forecasts of your people. When you click on the pencil icon next to the forecast number for one of your direct reports, you will see your management override options.

To override your Forecast, you'll need **Override Forecasts** permission.

This feature is available in:

✔ Unlimited	✔ Developer
✔ Enterprise	Group
✔ Professional	Personal

Task E   Submitting your forecast

You can view your own forecast, and that of any of your direct reports, by simply clicking on the Forecasts tab. These forecast amounts will not be reflected in any reports that anyone in your organization might run until you submit your forecast. Once you click submit, those numbers will be available in reports and in the Forecast History view.

To submit a forecast:

1. Click on the Forecasts tab to go to the Forecasts home page.
2. Click the Submit button and click OK.
3. You will now be seeing your forecast as submitted.
4. Click on the Forecasts tab to return to the Forecast view where you can see the forecasts and opportunities, as well as override your forecast.
5. Click the Forecast History button to see the snapshots of the forecasts you have submitted over time.

Submitting your forecast is like taking a snapshot of your forecast. How often you and your team members need to submit depends on how often your organization runs forecast reports.

If your company runs forecast reports every Friday afternoon for a Monday morning sales meeting, you probably want to update and submit your forecast on Friday morning.

This feature is available in:

- ✔ Unlimited
- ✔ Enterprise
- ✔ Professional
- ✔ Developer
- Group
- Personal

Chapter 5

List Views

- Understanding list views
- Using list views

Understanding list views

As your database grows, it can be difficult to find information—that's where list views come in. A list view allows you to see just the data you want to see—so, if you only want to see leads in San Francisco, you can create a list view of San Francisco leads. List views are available on almost every tab so you can slice and dice your database quickly and easily.

Task A   Identifying list views

A list view is a great way to organize your data so you can see smaller portions of your database. List views are designed to make you more productive, as you are only seeing the data that you need based on the criteria you set up.

To view a list view:

1.   Click on the Leads tab.
2.   Click the View drop-down and choose the view you'd like to see. For example, you could choose the All Open Leads view.
3.   The resulting list view will show all of the open leads that are assigned to you in Salesforce.

List views are a great way to organize your contacts before heading out on the road. Let's say you are heading to Los Angeles. You could create a list view for Los Angeles for leads, accounts, and opportunities. The resulting lists should help you build an itinerary that maximizes your time and efforts.

To view a list view, you'll need **Read** permission on **the current record type**. Examples of current record types are: contacts, accounts, leads, opportunities, etc.

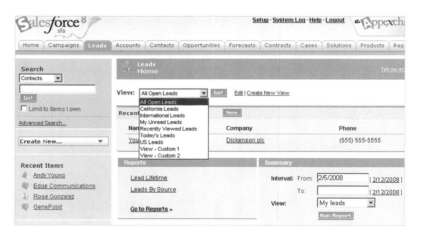

This feature is available in:

✔ Unlimited   ✔ Developer

✔ Enterprise   ✔ Group

✔ Professional   ✔ Personal

Task B Identifying tabs that have list views

Almost all of the tabs in Salesforce have list views. Each of these views is specific for that tab—so you will find different views depending on the type of information you are viewing.

To view tabs that have list views:

1. Click on the Leads tab. Some of the great views that are available in this view are: All Open Leads, Today's Leads, Unread Leads, and Recently Viewed Leads.
2. Click on the Accounts tab. Here, you can see views like: Recently Viewed Accounts, New Accounts, and Top Accounts.
3. Click on the Contacts tab. Here, you can see a lot of the same views found in the Accounts and Leads tabs. The Contacts tab also has things like Birthdays This Month. Send your customers a birthday card, and they will know you care enough to remember.
4. Click on the Opportunities tab. Here, you can easily stay on top of your business opportunities using list views like Closing This Month, New Opportunities, and Recently Viewed.
5. Click on other tabs in Salesforce. Depending on the version of Salesforce that you have, you can see list views in the following tabs: Campaign, Contracts, Cases, Solutions, and Products.

Grouping data together by job title can be a great way to focus sales efforts. For example, if your company has developed a product/solution that will save your customers money, looking at a list view based on the job title of CFO, Treasurer, or Controller can give you a new target list of prospects to contact.

To view a list view, you'll need **Read** permission on **the current record type**.

This feature is available in:

✔ Unlimited	✔ Developer
✔ Enterprise	✔ Group
✔ Professional	✔ Personal

Using list views

List views allow you to group your data together based on like-kind information. So, for example, you can create list views based on geography, area codes, job titles, etc. Anything you can query can be turned into a list view.

Task A   Viewing default list views

The default list views will give you a good idea of what can be done with list views. Use these list views to come up with ideas so you can create your own custom views.

To view the default list views:

1. Click on the Opportunities tab.
2. Click the View drop-down and choose the Closing Next Month view.
3. You will see the list of opportunities that are scheduled to close next month.
4. You can sort this list by clicking on any of the column headers. By clicking on that same column header again, you reverse the sort order.
5. Click any opportunity to bring up specific opportunity information, or click the Printable View link in the upper-right corner of Salesforce to print the list.

By looking at an opportunities list view for opportunities that will be closing next month, you can review what is needed to make sure you are on track. This is the perfect time to realign expectations if the deal isn't going to close or make a call to the prospect to keep things going right.

To view a list view, you'll need **Read** permission on **the current record type**.

This feature is available in:

✔ Unlimited   ✔ Developer
✔ Enterprise   ✔ Group
✔ Professional ✔ Personal

Task B   Creating custom list views

Creating custom list views allows you to tailor the database for your specific needs. You can group information together based on any of the fields in your database.

To create a custom list view for contacts:

1. Click on the Contacts tab.
2. Click on the Create New View link.
3. In Step 1, give your view a name.
4. In Step 2, choose whether you want to restrict the information to My Contacts or All Contacts.
5. In Step 3, choose to restrict the view results to a specific marketing campaign.
6. In Step 4, set up the search criteria. For the first column, choose Mailing City. (Or choose your default city field. Depending on how your database has been customized, this field name may be different.) For the second column, you can choose equals. For the third column, type a city name. For more information on the search criteria, see Task C in this section.
7. In Step 5, select the data you want to see in your report.
8. In Step 6, choose who can see this view.
9. Click Save to save your list view.

When creating a custom list view based on information that has different possible results, make sure to add all possible values to your query. For example, San Francisco could also be entered as SF, San Fran, or San Francisco.

A great way to create a custom list view for a geographic area is to use zip codes. If you do this, make sure your search criteria uses the starts with operator. For San Francisco, you could choose the (starts with) zip code of 941, which would give you all contacts that have a zip code starting with 941.

To create a list view, you'll need **Read** permission on **the current record type**.

To create, edit, or delete public list views, you'll need **Manage Public List Views** permission.

This feature is available in:

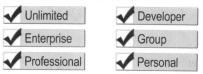

✔ Unlimited   ✔ Developer

✔ Enterprise   ✔ Group

✔ Professional   ✔ Personal

Task C   Entering search criteria

Setting up the search criteria can often be the most challenging part of creating a list view. If you don't get the results you think should be in your list view, you can always go back and edit the view until you get the query right.

To create the search criteria for a list view:

1. From the View drop-down, choose the view you'd like to edit and click the Edit link. If you would like to create a new list view, click the Create New View link.

2. (Note: This task assumes that you have completed step 1. Steps in this task are for step 2 only.) The first column shows a drop-down list of the fields that are available for searching. Choose the field you want to search on.

3. The second column shows the list of operators. Operators are used to connect the first column of information to the third column of information. For example, if the first column of information is the Annual Sales field and the last column is $500,000, the operator can be equal, less than, greater than, etc. So if you want to see Annual Sales greater than $500,000, you would choose greater than as the operator.

4. The third column shows the information you want to find. You can add up to 10 different search criteria. So, if you want to search on Annual Sales greater than $500,000, you would enter 500000 in this field.

5. The default setting that ties each search criteria together is AND. You can change this by clicking the Advanced Options.

6. Once you have completed your changes, click the Save button.

You can use relative date values when entering the search criteria. Examples include YESTERDAY, TODAY, TOMORROW, LAST WEEK, THIS WEEK, NEXT WEEK, LAST MONTH, THIS MONTH, etc. Each of these dates and times is based on the company profile that has been set up by your administrator.

Figuring out Boolean logic can be a full time job. A great way to learn more on how to create these search criteria is to Google Boolean logic. You will find many helpful websites with examples.

To create a list view, you'll need **Read** permission on **the current record type**.

To create, edit, or delete public list views, you'll need **Manage Public List Views** permission.

This feature is available in:

✔ Unlimited   ✔ Developer

✔ Enterprise   ✔ Group

✔ Professional   ✔ Personal

Task D Editing a list view

As your database changes and grows, it can become necessary to change how you view that data. Whether you are adding a new field to a list view or changing the criteria in a list view, knowing how to edit a list view is an important skill to have.

To edit a list view:

1. Click on the tab of the view you want to edit. For example, you could go to the Contacts tab to edit a list view that contains contact information.
2. Click on the View drop-down and choose the view you want to edit.
3. Make any changes to the list view.
4. Once your changes have been made, click the Save button.

If the view you are trying to create is similar to an existing view, click on the existing list view and then edit it. Once you have made the changes, click Save As and save the list view with a new name.

To edit a list view, you'll need **Read** permission on **the current record type**.

To create, edit, or delete public list views, you'll need **Manage Public List Views** permission.

This feature is available in:

✔ Unlimited	✔ Developer
✔ Enterprise	✔ Group
✔ Professional	✔ Personal

Task E   Deleting a list view

Sometimes it is just easier to delete a view and start over. Maybe you created a view for an event that has passed. Maybe there are views from a former employee.

If you are an administrator or a user with the Manage Public list views permission, you can delete shared views—including some of the standard views.

To delete a list view, you'll need **Read** permission on **the current record type**.

To delete public list views, you'll need **Manage Public List Views** permission.

To delete a list view:

1. Click on the tab that houses the list view you'd like to delete.
2. Click the View drop-down and choose the view you want to delete.
3. Click the Delete button at the top of the page.
4. Click OK to delete that view.

This feature is available in:

✓ Unlimited	✓ Developer
✓ Enterprise	✓ Group
✓ Professional	✓ Personal

Task F   Printing a list view

You are heading out on a road trip and need to print some critical contact information. If you have created a list view for the appropriate geography, you can print that list and take it with you.

To print a list view:

1. Click on the tab that houses the list view you'd like to print.
2. Click the View drop-down and choose the view you want to print.
3. If you want the data sorted before printing, click on the column header for your sort field.
4. Click the Printable View link in the upper-right corner of Salesforce.
5. Select the number of records you want to print—you can print up to 1,000 records at a time.
6. Click the Print This Page button. This will open your standard Windows Print dialog box.

To view a list view, you'll need **Read** permission on **the current record type**.

To print a list view, you'll need **Read** permission on **the current record type**.

								Number of records	15 ▼

All Open Leads
Displaying records 1 - 15

Number of records: 15 ▼
15
250
500
750
1000

Name ∧	Company	State/Province	Email	Lead Status	Created Date	Owner Alias	Unread By Ov
Akin, Kristen	Aethna Home Products	VA	kakin@athenahome.com	Working - Contacted	1/9/2008	CGill	✓
Bair, Betty	American Banking Corp.	PA	bblair@abankingco.com	Working - Contacted	1/9/2008	CGill	✓
Boxer, Bertha	Farmers Coop. of Florida	FL	bertha@fcof.net	Working - Contacted	1/9/2008	CGill	✓
Braund, Mike	Metropolitan Health Services	MD	likeb@metro.com	Open - Not Contacted	1/9/2008	CGill	✓
Brownell, Shelly	Western Telecommunications Corp.	CA	shellyb@westerntelecom.com	Working - Contacted	1/9/2008	CGill	✓
Cotton, Phyllis	Abbott Insurance	VA	pcotton@abbottins.net	Open - Not Contacted	1/9/2008	CGill	✓
Eberhard, Sandra	Highland Manufacturing Ltd.	CA	sandra_e@highland.net	Working - Contacted	1/9/2008	CGill	✓
Feager, Patricia	International Shipping Co.	NC	patricia_feager@is.com	Working - Contacted	1/9/2008	CGill	✓
Glimpse, Jeff	Jackson Controls		jeffg@jackson.com	Open - Not Contacted	1/9/2008	CGill	✓
James, Tom	Delphi Chemicals	MN	tom.james@delphi.chemicals.com	Working - Contacted	1/9/2008	CGill	✓

This feature is available in:

✔ Unlimited   ✔ Developer
✔ Enterprise   ✔ Group
✔ Professional   ✔ Personal

Chapter 6

Managing Activities

- Scheduling events and tasks
- Viewing activities
- Completing activities

Scheduling events and tasks

Scheduled events go on your calendar, and tasks show up in your task list. You can think of events as meetings. Tasks are to-dos.

When you schedule events or tasks in Salesforce, you can link them with just about any entity—like contacts, leads, accounts, etc.

Then, when you're on a contact record, you'll see all of the past events or completed tasks in the Activity History related list.

Task A   Scheduling a task

The next time you need to remind yourself to do something, leave your sticky notes in the drawer and schedule a task in Salesforce. Scheduled tasks can be linked with contacts, leads, accounts, or opportunities.

To schedule a task:

1. Go to the Home page. (Click the Home tab.)
2. Scroll down to the My Tasks section and click the New button.
3. Alternatively, you could choose the Task option from the Create New drop-down on the left column of Salesforce.
4. Enter details for your task.
5. Click OK.

Depending on how your organization is configured, you may be able to work with activities in the Console. Look at the list of tabs, and if you see a Console tab, check it out. The Console feature is only available in Professional, Enterprise, Unlimited, and Developer Editions.

To schedule a task, you'll need **Read** permission on **the record associated with the task**. You'll also need **Edit Tasks** permission.

This feature is available in:

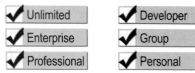

✔ Unlimited	✔ Developer
✔ Enterprise	✔ Group
✔ Professional	✔ Personal

Task B — Scheduling an event

Events are activities on your calendar that require a physical presence some-where. Unlike tasks, events have a duration and occupy a specific time slot on the calendar.

They could be meetings, webinars, conference calls, or just about any other type of business activity. They tend to occupy a specific time space on your calendar, and they usually involve one or more contacts or accounts in Salesforce.

To schedule an event:

1. Go to the Home page. (Click the Home tab.)
2. Scroll down to the Calendar section and click the New button.
3. Alternatively, you could choose the Event option from the Create New drop-down on the left column of Salesforce.
4. Enter details for your event.
5. Click OK.

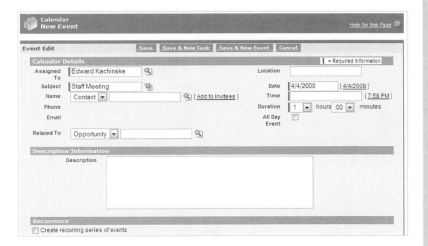

Events will appear in the Open Activities related list for the associated record. Once they have passed, they shift over to the Activity History related list.

Even if you have installed Connect for Microsoft Outlook, you will need to manually link activities in Outlook with a record in Salesforce for that event to show up on the Salesforce online calendar.

To schedule an event, you'll need **Read** permission on **the record associated with the event**. You'll also need **Edit Events** permission.

This feature is available in:

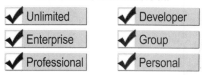

✔ Unlimited   ✔ Developer
✔ Enterprise   ✔ Group
✔ Professional   ✔ Personal

Task C   Inviting others to an event

You may have events that require the assistance of your colleagues. Maybe this takes the form of a staff meeting, a conference, or a major presentation for a client. Anytime you create an event in Salesforce, you can schedule it as a group event, and then it doesn't just show up on your calendar. It shows up on other users' calendars as well.

After scheduling a group event, other users will be able to either accept or decline the invitation to participate in the group event. Invitees are sent an e-mail, and the invitations also display on their home pages.

To schedule a group event, you'll need **Edit Events** permission.

To invite others to an event:

1. Go to the Home page. (Click the Home tab.)
2. Scroll down to the Calendar section and click the New button.
3. Alternatively, you could choose the Event option from the Create New drop-down on the left column of Salesforce.
4. Enter details for the activity.
5. Near the bottom of the event page, click the Add Invitees button.
6. Choose or find the users, leads, or contacts you'd like to invite. After selecting your invitees, click the Insert Selected button and click Done.
7. Click the Save & Send Update button at the top of the event page.

Calendar Select Event Invite

Search within Users, Leads & Contacts ▾ for betty   Go!

Search Results   Insert Selected Done Cancel

	Name	Title	Account/Company	Type	Owner
☑	Betty Bair	VP, Administration	American Banking Corp.	Lead	Edward Kachinske
☑	Betty Bair	VP, Administration	American Banking Corp.	Lead	Edward Kachinske
☐	Betty Smith			Contact	Edward Kachinske

Selected List

This feature is available in:

✔ Unlimited   ✔ Developer
✔ Enterprise   ✔ Group
✔ Professional   Personal

Task D   Scheduling recurring events

If the activity is so much fun—like a staff meeting—that you want to do it every week, you can schedule the activity as a recurring event. Recurring events are very similar to regular events; they just happen on a pre-defined regular interval.

To schedule a recurring event:

1. Click the Home tab.
2. Scroll down to the Calendar section and click the New button.
3. Alternatively, you could choose the Event option from the Create New drop-down on the left column of Salesforce.
4. Enter details for the activity, and make sure the Create recurring series of events checkbox is checked.
5. Select a frequency.
6. Click the Save button.

There is a limit to how many recurrences of the activity you can have. For example, a daily recurring activity can be scheduled for a maximum of 100 days.

To schedule a recurring activity, you'll need **Edit Events** permission.

Recurrence
☑ Create recurring series of events

Frequency	
◉ Daily	◉ Every weekday
○ Weekly	○ Every 1 days
○ Monthly	
○ Yearly	

Start Date 4/4/2008 [4/4/2008]
End Date   4/5/2008 [4/4/2008]

Reminder
Reminder ☑ 15 minutes ▼

Save   Save & New Task   Sav

This feature is available in:

✔ Unlimited	✔ Developer
✔ Enterprise	✔ Group
✔ Professional	✔ Personal

Viewing activities

There are two basic activity types in Salesforce: events and tasks. Events are the activities that show up on your calendar. An example of an event might be a meeting with a client. Tasks are to-dos that you set for contacts, leads, accounts, or opportunities. You might set a task to remind yourself to send a marketing package to a lead.

Task A   Navigating to your calendar

The easiest way to get to the Salesforce calendar is through the Home page. This is the page that appears when you first log into Salesforce, and you can easily get there at any point by clicking the Home tab.

To view activities on your Home page:

1. Go to the Home page. (Click the Home tab.)
2. Locate the Calendar section of the Home page.
3. Click the daily button to view your daily calendar. Next to the daily button, there is also a weekly and monthly button to navigate to the other base calendar views. You'll find these buttons under the mini calendar on the right side of the page.

If you don't see your activities on the Home page, scroll down a bit. It's probably near the bottom of your Home page. If you still can't find the links to your calendar, check with your administrator.

In any calendar view, click the Printable View link to print the calendar.

Every user has permission to see at least his/her calendar. To view an activity, you'll need to be the person assigned to the activity, or you'll need to be above that person in the role hierarchy. If you have the **View All Data** permission, you'll be able to see all activities. You'll also be able to see an activity if the contact, account, lead, or opportunity associated with the activity is viewable.

This feature is available in:

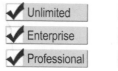

✔ Unlimited   ✔ Developer
✔ Enterprise   ✔ Group
✔ Professional   ✔ Personal

Task B Viewing event details

After scheduling an activity, you can bring up details for that activity by clicking the name of the activity on your calendar.

To view details for an activity:

1. Go to the Home page. (Click the Home tab.)
2. Locate the Calendar section of the Home page.
3. Click the daily button to view your daily calendar.
4. Locate the event. Click the name of the event, and a list of details for that event will appear.

While you are editing an activity, you can click the Create Follow Up Task and Create Follow Up Event buttons to create follow-up activities.

You can also hover your mouse over any event on the calendar to see details for that activity.

To view an activity, you'll need to be the person assigned to the activity, or you'll need to be above that person in the role hierarchy. If you have the **View All Data** permission, you'll be able to see all activities. You'll also be able to see an activity if the contact, account, lead, or opportunity associated with the activity is viewable.

This feature is available in:

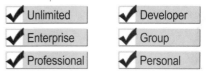

Task C   Viewing tasks

Almost every businessperson has had something slip through the cracks. Maybe you forgot to send someone a package. Perhaps you were supposed to send someone a follow-up note. No matter what is on your to-do list, you won't forget anything if it is on your task list in Salesforce.

To view tasks:

1. Go to the Home page. (Click the Home tab.)
2. Scroll down to the My Tasks section.
3. In the top-right corner of the My Tasks section, choose the tasks you'd like to see. For example, you could just look at the overdue tasks.
4. All of the tasks for the view that you've selected will appear.

Click the name of a task to bring up details for that task.

Tasks don't occupy a specific time slot on your calendar. They just occur on a specific day.

To view activities for multiple users, click the multi-user view icon on the Home page. You could also create a custom list view to show activities for just a specific user.

To view an activity, you'll need to be the person assigned to the activity, or you'll need to be above that person in the role hierarchy. If you have the **View All Data** permission, you'll be able to see all activities. You'll also be able to see an activity if the contact, account, lead, or opportunity associated with the activity is viewable.

My Tasks		New		Overdue	⏷
Complete	Date	Subject		Name	Related To
X		Check the ADN site for upcoming developer events and new programs.			
X		Visit the ADN Discussion Boards and post a question.			
X		Review the Apex Platform Getting Started.			
X		Download the toolkit of your choice from the Apex Wiki.			
X		Test task		John Doe, Acme Plumbing	
X		Send her a letter		Kristen Akin, Aethna Home Products	

Completing activities

When you're looking at a list of tasks, you'll need to know which ones are complete. As soon as you've completed a task, you should close that task in Salesforce. For events, the system will assume that an event has been completed as soon as the scheduled time for the event passes.

Task A   Closing a task

As soon as you finish a task, you should close it in Salesforce. Doing this changes the status for the task to Completed, and the task also then shows up in the Activity History related list for the linked record.

To close a task:

1. Go to the Home page. (Click the Home tab.)
2. Scroll down to the My Tasks section.
3. Locate the Complete column, and click the X in that column for the task you'd like to close.
4. The task-editing screen will appear. You'll notice that the status is automatically changed to Completed.
5. Edit any last minute information for the task and click the Save button.

When you close a task, the task will show up in the Activity History related list for the linked record. If you don't see the task, click the View All link to show all items in the related list.

To close a task, you'll need **Edit Tasks** permission. You'll also need to be: 1) the person assigned to the activity or 2) above that person in the role hierarchy, or 3) someone with **View All Data** permission, or 4) someone who has at least **Read** access for the record associated with the activity.

This feature is available in:

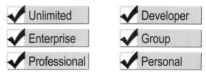

✔ Unlimited	✔ Developer
✔ Enterprise	✔ Group
✔ Professional	✔ Personal

Task B Deleting an event

Every once in a while, you will need to delete an event. Deleted events are completely removed from the database, so this is a procedure you'd run when you want to remove all record that the activity was ever scheduled.

Deleted events aren't permanently deleted. Instead, they are sent to the Recycle Bin for 30 days or until your Recycle Bin reaches its capacity limit, whichever comes first.

To delete an event, you'll need **Edit Events** permission. You'll also need to be: 1) the person assigned to the activity, or 2) above that person in the role hierarchy, or 3) someone with **View All Data** permission, or 4) someone who has at least **Read** access for the record associated with the activity.

To delete an event:

1. Go to the Home page. (Click the Home tab.)
2. Locate the Calendar section of the Home page.
3. Click the daily button to view your daily calendar.
4. Locate the event. Click the name of the event, and a list of details for that event will appear.
5. Click the Delete button.
6. Click Yes to confirm.

This feature is available in:

✔ Unlimited   ✔ Developer
✔ Enterprise   ✔ Group
✔ Professional   ✔ Personal

Chapter 7

Sending Emails

- Sending emails
- Sending mass emails
- Working with email templates

Sending emails

If you are using either the Personal or Group editions of Salesforce, you will not be able to send mass emails, but you can still send single emails. The single emails sent in the tasks in this chapter all are sent from within the Salesforce online interface. You can also set Salesforce to work with Outlook (covered in Chapter 14).

Task A   Sending a single free-form email

You can send emails to your leads, person accounts, and accounts from within Salesforce. A nice benefit of sending the emails from within Salesforce is that the system can keep a log of the sent email.

To send a single email to a contact or lead:

1. Go to a record. For this example, you might click on the Contacts tab to bring up the details for a contact record.
2. Scroll down to the Activity History related list.
3. Click the Send An Email button at the top of the Activity History related list.
4. Edit the subject and body of your message.
5. Click the Send button.

Salesforce will not allow you to send unlimited emails. Each edition has a maximum number of email addresses per day that can receive email messages from your organization:

> Unlimited Edition: 1,000 per day
> Enterprise Edition: 500 per day
> Professional Edition: 250 per day

If you need to send emails to more than 1,000 people per day, you should check out the AppExchange, where there are a number of mass emailing and email marketing applications.

> To send email, you'll need **Send Email** permission.

This feature is available in:

✔ Unlimited	✔ Developer
✔ Enterprise	✔ Group
✔ Professional	✔ Personal

Task B Sending a template-based email

Template-based email messages use the text of a pre-defined template as the body of the message. If you find that your staff is writing the same responses to contacts over and over, you'll probably save some time by creating a template. Then, the next time your coworkers send an email to a contact, you won't have to re-create the contents of the message.

To send a template-based email to a contact or lead:

1. Go to a record. For this example, you might click on the Contacts tab to bring up the details for a contact record.
2. Scroll down to the Activity History related list.
3. Click the Send An Email button at the top of the Activity History related list.
4. At the bottom of the message, click the Select Template button.
5. Choose an email template.
6. Modify any content from the resulting email.
7. Click the Send button to send the message.

You can create your own templates for use with single and mass emails. Creating templates is covered later in this chapter.

To send a template-based email, you'll need **Send Email** permission.

```
https://na5.salesforce.com - Select a Template - Mozilla Firefox     _ □ ×

Folder [ Unfiled Public Email Templates ▾ ]

Name                          Type  Description
Marketing: Product Inquiry    Text  Standard email response to website product inquiries
Response
Sales: New Customer Email     Text  Email to new customers
SUPPORT: Self-Service New     Text  Sample email template that can be sent to your
Comment Notification                Self-Service customers to notify them a public comment
(SAMPLE)                            has been added to their case.
SUPPORT: Self-Service New     Text  Notification of login and password to new Self-Service
User Login Information               user
(SAMPLE)
SUPPORT: Self-Service Reset   Text  Notification of new password when Self-Service
Password (SAMPLE)                   password is reset
Support: Case Assignment      Text  Notification to rep when case is auto-assigned
Notification
Support: Case Created (Phone  Text  Notification to customer about case created through
Inquiries)                          phone call
Support: Case Created (Web    Text  Notification to customer about case created online
Inquiries)
Support: Case Response        Text  Standardized template for responses to customer
                                    inquiries
Support: Escalated Case       Text  Notification email on case escalation
Notification

Done                                                      na5.salesforce.com
```

This feature is available in:

✔ Unlimited	✔ Developer
✔ Enterprise	✔ Group
✔ Professional	✔ Personal

Task C   Attaching files to an outgoing email

You may want to send a quote, invoice, letter, or other document with your email message. You can add attachments to any outgoing message.

Attachments are limited to 10 megabytes per file.

At the top of the attachment window, click the Search in Documents button to send a file that is in your Salesforce document library.

To send email with attachments, you'll need **Send Email** permission.

To attach a file to an outgoing email message:

1. Go to a record. For this example, you might click on the Contacts tab to bring up the details for a contact record.
2. Scroll down to the Activity History related list.
3. Click the Send An Email button at the top of the Activity History related list.
4. Edit the subject and body of your message.
5. Click the Attach File button.
6. Click the Browse button and locate the file you'd like to attach.
7. Click the Attach to Email button. When the attachment appears in the attachment list, click the Done button.
8. Click the Send button to send your message.

This feature is available in:

✔ Unlimited	✔ Developer
✔ Enterprise	✔ Group
✔ Professional	✔ Personal

Task D　Viewing the history of a sent email

You sent the email. You're sure you did. You just can't find it anywhere. If you sent it from within Salesforce, a copy of the email is conveniently stored in the Activity History related list for your email recipient.

To view the history of a sent email message:

1. Go to your contact, person account, or lead. So, for example, you could go to the Contacts tab and bring up the details for a specific contact record.
2. Once you have the details for your contact, person account, or lead on the screen, scroll down to your related lists for the contacts.
3. Under the Activity History related list, you should see a list of the email messages you have sent to this person.
4. You may need to click the View All button to scroll through all of the items in the Activity History related list.

Activity History	Log A Call	Mail Merge	Send An Email	Request Update	Activity History Help
	View All				

Action	Subject	Related To	Task	Due Date	Assigned To	Last Modified Date/Time
Edit	Del	Email: Hi Tammy		✓	3/16/2008	Edward Kachinske	3/16/2008 9:25 PM

Attachments are not retained in the Activity History related list.

To see the Activity History related list, you'll need **Read** permission on **the current record type**.

To log a history of the emails you send, you'll need **Edit** permission on **Tasks**.

This feature is available in:

✔ Unlimited　　✔ Developer
✔ Enterprise　　✔ Group
✔ Professional　✔ Personal

Task E   Setting your email signature

The email signature in Salesforce will be added to the bottom of each outgoing email sent from the online Salesforce interface. This signature is different from your Microsoft Outlook signature, if you are using Outlook as well as Salesforce.

To set your default email signature:

1. Click the Setup option in the upper-right corner of Salesforce.
2. On the left, choose the Email option.
3. Click My Email Settings.
4. Fill in the text of your email signature.
5. Click the Save button.

Attachments are limited to 10 megabytes per file.

At the top of the attachment window, click the Search in Documents button to send a file that is in your Salesforce document library.

To send email with attachments, you'll need **Send Email** permission.

My Email Settings		= Required Information

How would you like your name to appear on your outgoing email?

Email Name: `Edward Kachinske`

What email address would you like to use as your return address?

Email Address: `edward@is-crm.com`

Would you like to automatically BCC emails to your return address?

Automatic Bcc: ⦿ Yes ○ No

This signature will be added to your outgoing emails (1333 characters max):

Email Signature:

Note: All outgoing emails will contain a "Powered by Salesforce" tag line at the bottom. This tag can be removed in the paid Editions of the product.

Save   Cancel

This feature is available in:

✔ Unlimited   ✔ Developer
✔ Enterprise   ✔ Group
✔ Professional   ✔ Personal

Task F   Monitoring sent HTML emails

Whenever you send an HTML email message in Salesforce, a small one pixel (invisible) graphic is embedded into the outgoing message. When a person reads that email (which in most email clients automatically downloads pictures in the message), Salesforce sees that the email has been read. Wondering if your client has opened that email you sent? Salesforce will tell you.

To see if someone has read your email message:

1. Go to the details for the contact that was sent an HTML email message.
2. Scroll down to the HTML Email Status related list.
3. In this related list, you'll see the emails that are currently being tracked. You'll see when the message was sent, when it was first opened, when it was last opened, and the number of times the email has been opened.

Activity History		Log A Call	Mail Merge	Send An Email	Request Update	Activity History Help	
		View All					
Action	Subject		Related To	Task	Due Date	Assigned To	Last Modified Date/Time
Edit	Del	Email: Are you there?		sForce	✓	3/16/2008	Edward Kachinske	3/16/2008 1:49 PM
Edit	Del	Email: How are things?			✓	3/16/2008	Edward Kachinske	3/16/2008 12:54 PM
Edit	Del	Email: Just touching base			✓	3/16/2008	Edward Kachinske	3/16/2008 12:48 PM

Campaign History	Add Campaign	Campaign History Help
No records to display		

Notes & Attachments	New Note	Attach File	Notes & Attachments Help
No records to display			

HTML Email Status		Send An Email	View All	HTML Email Status Help
Action	Subject	Date Sent	Date Opened	# Times Opened	Last Opened
Edit	Del	Email: Are you there?	3/16/2008 1:49 PM	3/16/2008 1:59 PM	2	3/16/2008 2:00 PM

You will only see an HTML Email Status related list for a contact or a lead if you have sent that person an HTML email message and they have opened it.

To view the HTML Email Status related list for a contact, you'll need **Read** access on **Contacts** or **Leads**.

This feature is available in:

✔ Unlimited   ✔ Developer

✔ Enterprise   ✔ Group

✔ Professional   ✔ Personal

Sending mass emails

Chances are good that you've seen a mass email before. In fact, for many people, mass emails account for the vast majority of items in their inboxes. Salesforce lets you send small, targeted, and personalized mass emails.

Task A   Selecting recipients for your mass email (Mass email step 1)

Before you send a mass email, you'll need to create a list view that contains all of the recipients for the email. These instructions will show you the basics of how to do this, but you might also want to read Chapter 5 to learn more about configuring a list view.

To create a list view of recipients for your mass email:

1. Click on the Contacts tab.
2. In the Tools section, click the Mass Email Contacts option.
3. Click the Create New View option.
4. In Step 1, give the view a name.
5. In Step 2, set your filter. This is where you specify the contacts that should appear in the list view. If you, for example, choose "Contact: Mailing State/Province equals DC" then all of your DC contacts would appear in the list view.
6. Click the Save button.
7. Now that you have a list view that contains all of the intended recipients for the email, go to the next task.

Person accounts will appear in your contact list views.

You might want to add "Contact: Email contains @" to your list filter criteria. This will narrow the list to just contacts that have an email address.

To send email to leads, contacts, or person accounts, you'll need **Mass Email** permission.

To log a history of the emails you send, you'll also need **Edit Tasks** permission.

This feature is available in:

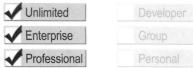

✔ Unlimited	Developer
✔ Enterprise	Group
✔ Professional	Personal

Step 1. Enter View Name | = Required Information

View Name: [   ]   (Example: "My Top Contacts")

Step 2. Specify Filter Criteria

Filter By Owner:
  ● All Contacts
  ○ My Contacts

Filter By Campaign (Optional):
  Campaign Name: [   ]

Advanced Filters Help

Filter By Additional Fields (Optional):

Field	Operator	Value	
--None--	--None--		AND
--None--	--None--		AND
--None--	--None--		AND
--None--	--None--		AND
--None--	--None--		

Advanced Options...

Step 3. Select Fields to Display

Available Fields
- Contact: Salutation
- Contact: First Name
- Contact: Last Name
- Contact: Mailing City
- Contact: Mailing State/Province
- Contact: Mailing Zip/Postal Code
- Contact: Mailing Country
- Contact: Other City

Selected Fields
- Contact: Name
- Contact: Email
- Account: Account Name

Add

Top / Up

Task B Choosing an email template (Mass email step 2)

This task is part of a sequence. If you haven't read the previous task yet, do so now. At this point in the mass email process, you should have created a list view to narrow the recipient list for the email blast.

To choose a mass email template:

1. Follow the steps in the previous task.
2. Once the list of mass email recipients is up on the screen, click the Next button in the upper-right corner.
3. A list of templates will appear. From the folder drop-down, you could choose a different folder to see other templates. Click the Preview option to see what any of the current templates look like.
4. Click the radio button to the left of the template you'd like to use.
5. Go to the next task in this book to continue the mass email process.

Attachments sent in mass emails appear as links. Files aren't physically attached, like you would expect to see if you had sent the message directly from Outlook.

🔒 To send email to leads, contacts, or person accounts, you'll need **Mass Email** permission.

🔒 To log a history of the emails you send, you'll also need **Edit Tasks** permission.

Step 2. Select an email template			Step 2 of 4

Previous | Next | Cancel

Please select an email template to use. To create a new template, you must exit this mass email process and create the new template in your personal setup section.

Folder [Unfiled Public Email Templates ▾]

Preview	Name	Type	Description
Preview	⦿ Marketing: Product Inquiry Response	Text	Standard email response to website product inquiries
Preview	○ Sales: New Customer Email	Text	Email to new customers
Preview	○ SUPPORT: Self-Service New Comment Notification (SAMPLE)	Text	Sample email template that can be sent to your Self-Service customers to notify them a public comment has been added to their case.
Preview	○ SUPPORT: Self-Service New User Login Information (SAMPLE)	Text	Notification of login and password to new Self-Service user
Preview	○ SUPPORT: Self-Service Reset Password (SAMPLE)	Text	Notification of new password when Self-Service password is reset
Preview	○ Support: Case Assignment Notification	Text	Notification to rep when case is auto-assigned

This feature is available in:

✔ Unlimited   Developer
✔ Enterprise   Group
✔ Professional   Personal

Task C   Setting processing and delivery options (Mass email step 3)

This task is part of a sequence. If you haven't read the previous task yet, go back to Task A now. At this point in the mass email process, you have already specified email recipients, and you've selected an email template. Now all you have to do is specify delivery options and click the Send button.

To set processing and delivery options for your mass email:

1. Follow the steps in Task A and Task B, the previous two tasks.
2. Select the following options: BCC me on one message, Store an activity for each message, and Use my signature.
3. Specify a name for this mass email.
4. Select when you'd like to send the massemail.
5. You can send it now, or you can choose to send it at a specific time in the future.
6. Click the Send button.

Your daily limit for mass email messages is calculated by UTC/GMT. So from midnight to midnight in Greenwich Mean Time, you are restricted to sending either 250, 500, or 1,000 messages—depending on the edition of Salesforce you have purchased.

Trial accounts cannot send mass emails.

You will receive an automatic status email from Salesforce for each mass email sent from your account.

To send email to leads, contacts, or person accounts, you'll need **Mass Email** permission.

To log a history of the emails you send, you'll also need **Edit Tasks** permission.

Step 3. Review and confirm   Step 3 of 4

Previous   Send   Cancel

You currently have **21 recipient(s)** selected to receive this email.

Processing Options | = Required Information

BCC me on one message   ☑

Store an activity for each message   ☑

Use my signature   ☐

Mass Email Name   [   ]

Delivery Options

◉ Send now

○ Schedule for delivery on [3/16/2008 9:30 PM]   Time Zone

[(GMT-08:00) Pacific Daylight Time (America/Los_Angeles) ▾]

Previous   Send   Cancel

This feature is available in:

✔ Unlimited   Developer
✔ Enterprise   Group
✔ Professional   Personal

Task D   Canceling a mass email

Whoops. You didn't mean to send that mass email. You're probably in a panic right now wondering how to cancel the message in Salesforce before it goes out to all of your customers. This task will show you how to cancel a mass email.

To cancel a mass email:

1. Click the Setup link at the top of Salesforce.
2. On the left, choose the Email option and then choose My Mass Emails.
3. Click the Cancel link next to the pending mass email you'd like to delete.

If the mass email has already started sending, you can click the Stop option to stop a mass email that is in the process of going out to your contacts.

Click the Del option next to a mass email to remove it from your queue. You can only delete sent or cancelled mass emails.

To cancel a mass email, you'll need **Modify All Data** permission.

This feature is available in:

✔ Unlimited	Developer
✔ Enterprise	Group
✔ Professional	Personal

Working with email templates

You send the same responses over and over. After meeting with a client, you send a follow-up message. After getting a specific request from a customer, you send a message. You get into the same situation often, and instead of creating an individual response, create your response as a template. Then, the next time you have a client meeting, you can send a standard follow-up email.

Task A Viewing and editing email templates

To view a list of your email templates, you'll have to go to the setup area of Salesforce.

To view an email template:

1. Click the Setup link in the upper-right corner of Salesforce.
2. On the left, click the Email option.
3. Click My Templates. A list of your templates will appear.
4. To see other templates, choose a folder from the Folder drop-down.
5. Click the All button to view all available templates.
6. Click the name of an email template to view the details for the template.

Once you have the details of an email template up on the screen, click the Edit button to edit any part of the template. Click the Delete button to get rid of it. Click the Clone button to save the template with a new name.

To upload or edit templates, you'll need **Edit HTML Templates** permission.

To create or change public templates, you'll need **Manage Public Templates** permission.

Unfiled Public Email Templates   Help for this Page

Below is a list of all your email templates in the folder selected. Click the new button to create a new text or HTML email template. You can use these email templates for mass email and when sending single emails.

Folder [My Personal Email Templates ▼] Create New Folder

A | B | C | D | E | F | G | H | I | J | K | L | M | N | O | P | Q | R | S | T | U | V | W | X | Y | Z | Other **All**

New Template

Action	Email Template Name ⌃	Template Type	Available For Use	Description	Owner	Last Modified Date
Edit | Del	Marketing: Product Inquiry Response	Text	✓	Standard email response to website product inquiries	EKach	2/6/2008
Edit | Del	Sales: New Customer Email	Text	✓	Email to new customers	EKach	2/6/2008
Edit | Del	SUPPORT: Self-Service New Comment Notification (SAMPLE)	Text	✓	Sample email template that can be sent to your	EKach	2/6/2008

This feature is available in:

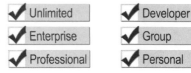

✔ Unlimited   ✔ Developer
✔ Enterprise   ✔ Group
✔ Professional ✔ Personal

Task B Using letterheads

Letterheads determine the default look and feel for your outgoing HTML email templates. You write the body of the email message each time you send it, but the letterhead determines the graphics and text at the bottom and the top of the message.

To create a new letterhead:

1. Click the Setup link in the upper-right corner of Salesforce.
2. On the left, click the Communication Templates option.
3. Click the Create or Update Your Company Letterheads option.
4. Click Next.
5. Click the New Letterhead option.
6. Give the letterhead a name and click Save.
7. Edit the background color, header, body, and footer for the letterhead.
8. Click the Save button.

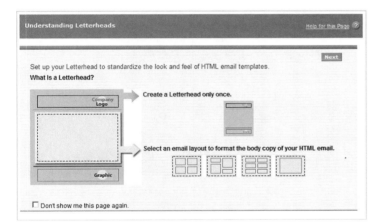

Letterheads are probably something that your administrator will configure for you.

To create letterheads, you'll need **Manage Letterheads** permission.

This feature is available in:

✔ Unlimited   ✔ Developer
✔ Enterprise   ✔ Group
✔ Professional   Personal

Within the body of your outgoing email template, you can add field placeholders to pull contact-specific data from the contact or lead record into the resulting email message. When you are designing the email template, look in the blue Available Merge Fields area for help on formatting the field placeholders.

To upload or edit templates, you'll need **Edit HTML Templates** permission.

Task C Creating a new email template

Creating a new email template will make it faster for you to respond to a single person or multiple people in the same kind of situation. Sending template-based messages is covered earlier in this chapter.

To create an HTML email template:

1. Click the Setup link in the upper-right corner of Salesforce.
2. On the left, click the Email option.
3. Click My Templates. A list of your templates will appear.
4. Click the New Template button.
5. Select to use a text-only template, an HTML template, or a custom template. HTML templates will use the letterhead feature, and custom templates do not add any formatting from your letterhead.
6. Click Next.
7. Add a folder, template name, character set, and subject for the email template. You can also add an email body.
8. Click the Save button.

Custom Email Template Edit
Edward's Template   Help for this Page

Paste the HTML code for your custom HTML email in the box below. Use merge fields to personalize your email content.
If the text version of the template is left blank, this version will be stripped of HTML and sent as the text version.

Available Merge Fields
Select Field Type   Select Field   Copy Merge Field Value
Contact Fields   ▾   ▾
Copy and paste the merge field value into your HTML content below.

Step 3. Create HTML version   Step 3 of 4

                                    Preview   Previous   Next   Cancel

HTML Email Content | = Required Information
                    Subject ‖
                  HTML Body

This feature is available in:

✔ Unlimited   ✔ Developer
✔ Enterprise   ✔ Group
✔ Professional   ✔ Personal

Chapter 8

Writing Letters and Mail Merge

- Managing templates
- Standard versus extended mail merge

Managing templates

Facilitating communication with customers and prospects is an important feature of any customer relationship management system. A mail merge allows you to send the same letter document to multiple contacts, and personalize each communication with data from the contact's record in your database. This is all driven from the templates. Templates are Microsoft Word documents with placeholders for the field data that will be pulled from the records in Salesforce.

Task A   Installing the Microsoft Word integration

Since the template requires the use of Microsoft Word, you'll first need to install the integration between Word and Salesforce. It's a fairly straightforward process, called Force.com Connect for Microsoft Office, and it includes an add-in for both Word and Excel. The Excel integration is handy when it comes to reporting out of Salesforce.

To install the Microsoft Word integration:

1. On your local machine, close all open programs, and specifically you will need to close all Microsoft Office applications, including Word, Excel, and Outlook.
2. In Salesforce, click Setup, then under the Personal Setup section in the sidebar on the left, click Desktop Integration.
3. Click Connect for Microsoft Office.
4. Click Install Now or Yes.
5. You will now be in the installer wizard; click Next.
6. Click the I accept radio button and click Next.
7. Click Finish. You will have to restart your computer for the Connect for Office integration to be complete. Click Yes to restart immediately, or No to restart later.
8. When you open Microsoft Word, you should now see a Salesforce.com drop-down on the toolbar.

Currently, Force.com Connect for Office works with Microsoft Office 2000, XP/2002, 2003, and 2007. And it will run on the Microsoft Windows 2000, XP, or Vista operating systems, provided that they are 32-bit; 64-bit processors are not supported.

If you are wondering what in the heck a 64-bit processor is, it's basically technology that improves the speed of your computer, and back in the 1960s, it was only available in supercomputers. Advances in computing are bringing this faster processor to the desktop; however, many well known and loved (or not) applications cannot run on those faster processors.

To install the Connect for Office Integration, you will need to log into your computer with a user profile that has the rights to install software.

This feature is available in:

✔ Unlimited   ✔ Developer

✔ Enterprise   ✔ Group

✔ Professional   ✔ Personal

Task B Creating a Microsoft Word template for mail merge

Using the Salesforce Microsoft Word integration (Connect for Office), you can create mail merge templates, and then embed field placeholders from Salesforce into the mail merge template. When you select the contacts and run the mail merge, Salesforce will insert the data from the contact record into a Word document. Templates can be real time savers. If you find yourself writing the same content again and again, chances are it is a good candidate for a template. Then, when you want to send that document to a contact, you won't have to copy/paste or re-create the content.

To create a Microsoft Word template for mail merge:

1. Launch Microsoft Word and open a blank document.
2. Click on the Salesforce.com drop-down on the toolbar and select Log in. You will need to enter your username and password, with your security token appended to the end of your password.
3. Create the letter, and to insert field placeholders from Salesforce, click on the Salesforce.com drop-down on the toolbar and select Insert Merge Field.
4. First, you need to choose a field type from the list in the column on the left. Then you can select a field from the list of fields on the right. You can select multiple fields by simply clicking on each field, and then click Insert.
5. To enter information in the signature block at the end of the letter, select the User Fields field type, and then select Name, Company, Title, and Phone and those will pull the data from each user's record.
6. Save your Word document. For the steps to upload your template, see Task B in the Managing Templates section.

Every time you open or create a template in Word, you will have to log into Salesforce. Your typical Salesforce login, with your username and password, is not enough. You will need to generate a security token—a long code—from Salesforce that will be emailed to you. You will then append your password with this code to authenticate the external connection to Salesforce.

With the security token your login will look something like this:

username@domain.com

passwordalxiQM8hHYrQi2cmZdLA uu7rm

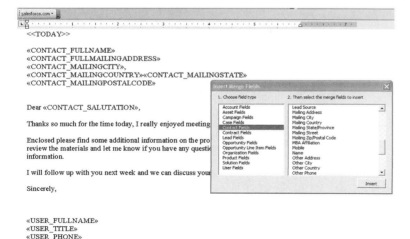

This feature is available in:

✔ Unlimited   ✔ Developer
✔ Enterprise   ✔ Group
✔ Professional   ✔ Personal

Task C   Uploading a Microsoft Word template to Salesforce

Preparing a template in Word to be used in Salesforce for mail merges is a two-step process. Step 1 is to create the template in Word, covered in Task B of this section. Step 2 is to upload that template to Salesforce so that you can use it in mail merges.

To upload a Microsoft Word template to Salesforce:

1. In Salesforce, click Setup | Administration Setup | Communication Templates | Mail Merge Templates.
2. You will see a list of existing mail merge templates, if any; click New Template.
3. Enter a name for your template and a description.
4. Click the Browse button to the right of the File field and browse to the location where you saved your Microsoft Word template. Click on the template and click Open Save.
5. Click Save.

There are some handy sample templates that you can download from the online User Guide. In Salesforce, click the Help link and then in the Search text field, search for "mm_templates.zip" (without the quotes). Download and extract the zip files and there will be 16 sample templates, including templates for Avery labels, # 10 envelopes, and several letters. There is also a handy Read Me document that covers how to use and upload the sample templates. There is even a Product Quote template that pulls the fields from the Contact record as well as the Opportunity record.

If you upload a template, then decide to make changes to that template, you'll need to make the changes in Word first, and then re-upload the template to Salesforce.

To upload Microsoft Word mail merge templates, you'll need **Manage Public Templates** permission.

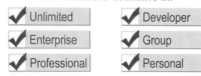

This feature is available in:

✔ Unlimited	✔ Developer
✔ Enterprise	✔ Group
✔ Professional	✔ Personal

Task D   Sending a letter to a contact

Now that you have created the template in Word and uploaded it to Salesforce, you can use that template to generate a letter to a contact. Once you create the letter, Salesforce will also initiate an activity history dialog box, so that you can record that you have sent a letter or document to that contact.

To send a letter to a contact:

1. First, go to the Contact view by clicking the Contacts tab and then searching for the contact to whom you want to send a letter.
2. In the Activity History section, click the Mail Merge button.
3. In step 1, confirm that the contact in the Record to Merge field is correct. To search for a different contact, click the lookup icon and search for the correct contact.
4. In step 2, select the mail merge template that you would like to use.
5. In step 3, clear the check box if you don't want to log the letter as an activity. This option is checked by default.
6. Click Generate.
7. Two things will happen: the merged document will open in Microsoft Word, and in Salesforce the Log a Call screen will open.
8. You can print and save the document in Microsoft Word.
9. In Salesforce, complete any of the information you want to add to the task and click Save. The task will be displayed in the Activity History section of the contact record.

If you are using the Mozilla Firefox web browser to access Salesforce, and you try to initiate a mail merge to Word from that browser, you will get a message that you are using an unsupported browser for mail merge. In order to use Mozilla, you'll have to get the extended mail merge feature activated. We cover that later in this chapter.

You might realize that you are saving the document you created locally, which can only be seen by you. If you want other users to see this document, you might want to consider attaching it to the contact. We cover that in Chapter 9.

**Task
Mail Merge**   Help for this Page

On this page you can generate a Microsoft Word document that includes your Contact data. Please select the recipient's name and choose a mail merge template.

1. Choose the record to merge:

   Jane Keene

2. Choose a mail merge template:

   Avery 5160 Label
   Meeting Follow Up
   New Template
   Opportunity Quote

3. ☑ Log an activity

   Generate   Cancel

This feature is available in:

✔ Unlimited   ✔ Developer
✔ Enterprise   ✔ Group
✔ Professional   ✔ Personal

Task E Including opportunity data in mail merge templates

Using Word templates for letter communication is great, but you can also take advantage of the opportunity data you have in Salesforce, and insert that data into a Word template as well. This lends itself well to creating a proposal or quote template in Word that you can send to prospects and customers, reflecting the data in the sales opportunity.

To include opportunity data in a mail merge template:

1. Launch Microsoft Word and open a blank document.
2. Click on the Salesforce.com drop-down on the toolbar and select Log in.
3. Create the content for the letter, and in the place where you want to insert an opportunity field, click on the Salesforce.com drop-down on the toolbar and select Insert Merge Field.
4. Select the Opportunity Fields field type to insert field placeholders from the Opportunity detail view.
5. To create a table of the opportunity products, choose Opportunity Line Item as the field type. Select all of the line item fields you want to insert by clicking on each field and then clicking Insert.
6. Complete the template in Word, save it, and upload it to Salesforce. The steps to upload a Word template to Salesforce are in Task C in the Managing Templates section in this chapter.

A template for a product quote that already has the opportunity field placeholders embedded in it is available from the online User Guide. In Salesforce, click the Help link and then in the Search text field, search for "mm_templates.zip" (without the quotes). Download and extract the zip files and you will find 16 sample templates, including a product quote template that pulls the fields from the Contact record as well as the Opportunity record.

To upload Microsoft Word mail merge templates, you'll need **Manage Public Templates** permission.

To view opportunities, you'll need **Read** permission on **Opportunities**.

To view opportunity products, you'll need **Read** permission on **Opportunities, Products**, and **Price Books**.

This feature is available in:

- ✓ Unlimited
- ✓ Developer
- ✓ Enterprise
- ✓ Group
- ✓ Professional
- ✓ Personal

Task F — Merging an opportunity template

Now that you have created a template in Word using the opportunity field placeholders, and the template is uploaded to Salesforce, you can use that template to generate a document to a contact, pulling some contact data, like name and address, and some opportunity data, like products, quantities, and amounts.

To merge an opportunity template:

1. Click on the Opportunities tab to go to the Opportunities home view.
2. Find the opportunity from which you would like to merge and click on the opportunity name.
3. Make sure that your opportunity has at least one contact linked to it in the Contact Roles section.
4. In the Activity History section, click Mail Merge.
5. In step 1, confirm opportunity record to merge is correct.
6. If you have more than one contact linked to this opportunity, then you will have a step 2, where you can choose which contact to merge.
7. In step 3, select the mail merge template that you would like to use.
8. In step 4, clear the check box if you don't want to log the letter as an activity. This option is checked by default.
9. Click Generate.

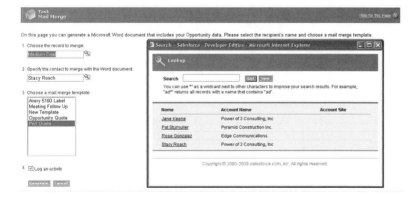

Once you have saved the document, like a proposal or quote, you might be thinking, "Hey, this is saved to my local computer. My colleagues aren't going to be able to open or view this great quote." And you'd be spot on.

If you want other users to see the document you just created and saved on your local machine, you should attach it to the opportunity record in Salesforce. In the opportunity record, scroll down to Notes & Attachments and click Attach file. Browse to the location where you saved the file locally and click Open; then click Attach File and Done.

To upload Microsoft Word mail merge templates, you'll need **Manage Public Templates** permission.

To view opportunities, you'll need **Read** permission on **Opportunities**.

To view opportunity products, you'll need **Read** permission on **Opportunities, Products**, and **Price Books**.

This feature is available in:

✔ Unlimited   ✔ Developer
✔ Enterprise   ✔ Group
✔ Professional   ✔ Personal

Standard versus extended mail merge

When you start using Salesforce, you will be using the standard mail merge interface. With this interface you will be limited to merging only one contact at a time. To perform a mass mail merge to multiple records, you will need to request the extended mail merge feature from Salesforce, as it is a by-request only feature. Prior to setting up extended mail merge, you will need to install the mail merge ActiveX control.

Task A   Using standard mail merge

The first time you generate a mail merge document using the standard mail merge, you will be prompted to set up the Mail Merge ActiveX Control. This lets Salesforce and Word talk beyond the interaction that Connect for Office provides, and it will allow you to merge single documents from contacts and opportunities.

To use the standard mail merge:

1. Open Internet Explorer 6 or 7.
2. Click Tools | Internet Options, then click on the Security tab.
3. Click on the icon for Internet and click the Custom Level button.
4. In the ActiveX controls and plug-in section, set the radio button to either Enable or Prompt for the following settings: Download signed ActiveX controls, Run ActiveX controls and plug-ins, and Script ActiveX controls marked safe for scripting. In the Downloads section, set the radio button to Enable for the File download setting and click OK.
5. Now click the icon for Trusted Sites, and click the Sites button. In the Add this website to the zone: type https://*.salesforce.com and click Add and OK.
6. Click on the Custom Level button and repeat Step 4 of this task.
7. Click on the Advanced tab, and in the Security section make sure that the Do not save encrypted pages to disk check box is not checked.
8. Click OK and then close and re-open Internet Explorer.

You have to be logged into Windows as a user with administrative privileges to download the ActiveX controls. If you don't have sufficient privileges, you may have to enlist your friendly neighborhood IT professional.

The ActiveX controls only work with Microsoft Internet Explorer 6 or 7; Windows 2000, XP, or Vista; and Word 2000, XP/2002, or 2007.

To install the Mail Merge ActiveX control, you need to log into your computer with a user profile that has Administrative privileges.

This feature is available in:

✔ Unlimited   ✔ Developer

✔ Enterprise   ✔ Group

✔ Professional   ✔ Personal

Task B Using extended mail merge

With extended mail merge, you can perform a mass mail merge to multiple records at once. In addition, you will be able to use the Mozilla Firefox browser and the Apple Mac OS to initiate mail merges in Salesforce. You will also be able to merge multiple records to envelopes and labels. Also, if you request and activate the extended mail merge feature, you will not have to install the ActiveX controls we covered in the previous task.

To set up extended mail merge:

1. Call Salesforce.com Customer Support at (415) 901-7010 or log a case in the Help and Training section of Salesforce.
2. Click Setup | App Setup | Customize | User Interface and click the check box for extended mail merge.
3. You can now use the feature of extended mail merge, such as mass mail merges and printing labels.

This process takes up to 48 hours to complete, so don't call Salesforce on the day you want to send a mass mail merge.

Extended mail merge does not support Word 2007 templates saved in .docx or .dotx formats, but Standard mail merge does support that format.

To request and activate extended mail merge, you'll need to be a Salesforce administrator.

This feature is available in:

✔ Unlimited   ✔ Developer
✔ Enterprise   ✔ Group
✔ Professional ✔ Personal

Task C   Sending mass mail merge

Mass mail merges can be great time savers and are a great way to send the same communication to multiple contacts from your Salesforce database. To complete a mass mail merge, you need to first create a template in Word with field placeholders to personalize the communication, upload it to Salesforce, and then select the records in Salesforce to whom you would like to send the communication. Pulling the trigger on the mass mail merge is the final step.

To send a mass mail merge:

1. You can initiate a mass mail merge for accounts, contacts, or leads. Click on the home tab for one of those options, such as Contacts.
2. In the Tools area, click Mass Mail Merge; the wizard will open.
3. Select a view from the View drop-down; you can also create a custom view. For more information on custom list views, see Chapter 5 of this book.
4. Click the check box for the records you want to include in the mail merge. To select all the records displayed on the page, click the check box in the column header at the top. Click Next.
5. Select the type of Word document you would like to create, such as a document, envelope, or label.
6. Click the Log Activity check box to record this task as completed in the Activity History section of the account, contact, or lead. Click Next.
7. Select the template you want to use for this mail merge. If you are generating a document, you can select whether to create a single Word document, or a separate document for each account, contact, or lead. You can click Preview Template to view the template.
8. Click Finish. You will be sent an email with the merged file attached when the merge is complete.

When you send a mail merge using extended mail merge, Salesforce will not open a Word document. It will either be emailed to you or you can send the completed mail merge to the Documents tab, so that any other users in your organization can also view the communication.

To send mass mail merges, you need the extended mail merge feature enabled.

To send a mass mail merge, you'll need **Read** permission on **Contacts**, **Accounts**, or **Leads** that you want to include in the merge.

This feature is available in:

✔ Unlimited ✔ Developer
✔ Enterprise ✔ Group
✔ Professional ✔ Personal

Task D   Printing labels

Another feature of extended mail merge is the ability to produce mailing labels for multiple contacts.

To print labels:

1. You can print labels via the mass mail merge for accounts, contacts, or leads. Click on the home tab for one of those options, such as Contacts.

2. In the Tools area, click Mass Mail Merge; the wizard will open.

3. Select a view from the View drop-down; you can also create a custom view. For more information on custom list views, see Chapter 5 of this book.

4. Click the check box next to the records for which you want to produce labels. To select all the records displayed on the page, click the check box in the column header at the top. Click Next.

5. Select label as the type of Word document you want to create.

6. Click the Log Activity check box to record this task as completed in the Activity History section of the account, contact, or lead. Click Next.

7. Select the label template you want to use for this mail merge. You can click Preview Template to view the label template.

8. Click Finish. You will be sent an email with the merged file attached when the label merge is complete, and you can then open that attachment and print the labels.

If you are reading this chapter all the way through, then you are not a typical sales person. You might have noticed that I have already mentioned some slick sample templates that you can download from the online User Guide. Well, there are templates in there for five of the standard Avery labels, as well as monarch and # 10 envelopes.

In Salesforce, click the Help link and then in the Search text field, search for "mm_templates.zip" (without the quotes). Download and extract the zip files and there will be 16 sample templates, including the label and envelope templates.

To send mass mail merges, you need the extended mail merge feature enabled.

To send a mass mail merge, you'll need **Read** permission on **Contacts**, **Accounts**, or **Leads** that you want to include in the merge.

This feature is available in:

✔ Unlimited	✔ Developer
✔ Enterprise	✔ Group
✔ Professional	✔ Personal

Chapter 9

Managing Documents

- Using the Document Library

Using the document library

The Document Library can be a great resource for collaboration within your organization. Important spreadsheets, sales collateral, technical documents, and more can all be shared with your coworkers using the Document Library.

Task A Uploading documents

Because Salesforce is an online tool, adding documents to the Document Library requires a quick upload. Of course, speed of your uploads depends on your connection to the Internet. Once uploaded, your document lives on the Salesforce servers and is accessible to all users who have access within your organization.

To upload a document to the Document Library:

1. Click the Documents tab.
2. Click the New button to create a new document. (If you are already in a folder, the button will say New Document.)
3. Click the New Document button.
4. Enter the document name, and make sure you put the document in the correct folder. Enter other optional information, like a description or keywords.
5. Click the Browse button and select a file to upload.
6. Click the Save button. Your document will upload to the folder you selected.

When uploading a document to the Document Library, you have the option to make that document Externally Available. Choosing this option gives you the ability to include the document in template-based emails to non-Salesforce users.

To open the documents tab, you'll need **Read** permission on **Documents**.

To upload new documents, you'll need **Create** permission on **Documents**.

To upload a new version of an existing document, you'll need **Edit** permission on **Documents**.

To view documents, you'll need **Read** permission on **Documents**.

This feature is available in:

✔ Unlimited ✔ Developer
✔ Enterprise ✔ Group
✔ Professional ✔ Personal

Upload New Document

1. Enter details   = Re
Document Name | [   ] New
Internal Use Only □
Externally Available □
Image
Folder My Personal Documents ▾
Description
[   ]
Keywords [   ]

2. Select the file
⊙ Enter the path of the file or click browse to find the file.
File to upload [   ] Browse...
Or:
○ Create a reference link to the file. Enter a file location that others can access.
Path/URL to reference [   ]

3. Click the "Save" button
Save

Task B   Viewing documents

A document list will display all documents in a folder. You can use this document list to download a document, edit its properties, or change information about the document. Think of document lists as an organizational tool that you can use to show a set of related documents.

To view documents:

1. Click the Documents tab.
2. From the Folder drop-down, choose the folder for the documents you want to view.
3. Click the Go! button.
4. Your document list will appear.

Click the name of a document in the document list to download the document.

Looking for a printout of your document list? Click the Printable View option on any document list.

To view documents, you'll need **Read** permission on **Documents**.

To edit documents, you'll need **Edit** permission on **Documents**.

Documents Home

Enter keywords to find matching documents.

[   ] Find Document

Document Folders

Folder [My Personal Documents ▼] Go!   Create New Folder

Recent Documents   New

Name	Description
Big Proposal	

This feature is available in:

✔ Unlimited	✔ Developer
✔ Enterprise	✔ Group
✔ Professional	✔ Personal

Task C   Creating a folder

If you have hundreds of documents in your Document Library, you'll definitely want to categorize the documents into folders.

You won't be able to have two folders with the same name.

To open the documents tab, you'll need **Read** permission on **Documents**.

To upload new folders, you'll need **Create** permission on **Documents**.

To view documents, you'll need **Read** permission on **Documents**.

To create a folder in the Document Library:

1. Click the Documents tab.
2. Click the Create New Folder link next to the Folder drop-down.
3. Enter a name for your folder, and specify the public access for the folder. (Read only or Read/Write.)
4. Select a level of access for the folder for other Salesforce users. The folder can be accessible by all users, hidden from all users, or accessible only by selected users or groups.
5. Click the Save button.

New Document Folder

Folder Edit   Save Cancel

Document Folder   Proposals
Public Folder Access   Read Only ▼

◉ This folder is accessible by all users
○ This folder is hidden from all users
○ This folder is accessible only by the following users:
Search: Public Groups   ▼   for: Find

Available for Sharing   Shared To
--None--   --None--

Add
▶

This feature is available in:

✔ Unlimited   ✔ Developer
✔ Enterprise   ✔ Group
✔ Professional   ✔ Personal

Task D   Searching for documents

If the document you want doesn't immediately appear, you can search for it. This feature is especially useful if you have a large organization with a long list of documents in your Document Library.

To search for a specific document:

1. Click the Documents tab.
2. Enter a keyword into the search area at the top of the Documents Home page.
3. Click the Find Document button.
4. A list of the documents containing your keyword will appear.

```
Documents
Home

Enter keywords to find matching documents.
proposals                    Find Document

Document Folders

Folder  Proposals        ▼  Go!   Edit | Create New Folder

Recent Documents        New

Name                          Description
Big Proposal
```

When searching for a specific document, you can search using one or more of the following fields:
- Document Name
- Keywords
- Description
- Type

To search for documents, you'll need **Read** permission on **Documents**.

This feature is available in:

✔ Unlimited	✔ Developer
✔ Enterprise	✔ Group
✔ Professional	✔ Personal

The following properties are recorded for each document:

- Author
- Created By
- Modified By
- Folder
- Document Name
- Description
- Internal Use Only
- Externally Available
- Keywords
- Path
- Size
- Type

🔒 To view documents, you'll need **Read** permission on **Documents**.

🔒 To edit the properties of documents, you'll need **Edit** permission on **Documents**.

Task E   Viewing properties of a document

Every document that is uploaded to Salesforce gets tagged with a number of predefined properties. These properties—like the document author, create date, and description—can help you identify the source and current status of any document in the Documents Library.

To view or edit the properties of a document:

1. Go to the Documents tab.
2. Find a document you'd like to email. Click the name of the document to bring up its properties.
3. Click the Edit Properties button to change the name, availability, folder, description, or keywords for the document.
4. Click the Save button to save any changes.

Document **Big Proposal**	Help for this Page

Document Detail   Edit Properties | Delete | Replace Document | Email Document

Document Name	Big Proposal
Internal Use Only	
Folder	My Personal Documents
Author	Edward Kachinske [Change]
File Extension	csv
MIME Type	application/vnd.ms-excel
Size	220KB
Description	
Keywords	
	Click here to view this file
Created By	Edward Kachinske, 4/2/2008 2:09 PM Modified By Edward Kachinske, 4/2/2008 2:09 PM

Edit Properties | Delete | Replace Document | Email Document

This feature is available in:

✔ Unlimited   ✔ Developer
✔ Enterprise   ✔ Group
✔ Professional ✔ Personal

Task F   Emailing a document

You may have a document in your Documents tab that you'd like to share with someone outside your group of Salesforce users. It's easy to email a document to anyone in the world.

To email a document:

1. Go to the Documents tab.
2. Find a document you'd like to email. Click the name of the document to bring up its properties.
3. Click the Email Document button.
4. Enter a recipient, subject, and body for your email.
5. Click the Send button.

While you are creating your outgoing message, click the Switch to HTML link to add formatting to the text of your outgoing message.

Click the Select Template button at the bottom of the email message to use a predefined template email as the basis for your message.

To email documents, you'll need **Read** permission on **Documents**.

Task
Send an Email

Send | Select Template | Attach File | Preview | Check Spelling | C

Edit Email

Email Format	HTML [Switch to Text-Only]
To	
Related To	Account
Additional To:	
CC:	
BCC:	edward@is-crm.com
Subject	
Body	Formatting Controls [How to use this] Font	Size	B I U

This feature is available in:

✔ Unlimited	✔ Developer
✔ Enterprise	✔ Group
✔ Professional	✔ Personal

Task G   Deleting documents

If you no longer need a document in the Document Library, you can delete it. Like most software today, Salesforce doesn't permanently delete this information; rather, it stores deleted documents in a Recycle Bin.

Be careful! While deleted documents do end up in the Recycle Bin, they only stay there for a few days. If you deleted something six months ago and are looking to restore it, the document will not be recoverable.

Click the green Recycle Bin icon on the lower-left corner of the Salesforce screen to view recently deleted documents.

To delete documents, you'll need **Delete** permission on **Documents**.

To delete a document:

1. Click the Documents tab.
2. Find a document you'd like to email. Click the name of the document to bring up its properties.
3. Click the Delete button.
4. Click Yes to confirm.

Document	Big Proposal	
Document Detail	Edit Properties	Delete	Replace
Document Name	Big Proposal	
Internal Use Only		
Folder	My Personal Documents	
Author	Edward Kachinske [Change]	
File Extension	csv	
MIME Type	application/vnd.ms-excel	
Size	220KB	

This feature is available in:

✔ Unlimited   ✔ Developer
✔ Enterprise   ✔ Group
✔ Professional   ✔ Personal

Chapter 10

Administering Campaigns

- Setting up campaigns
- Managing Campaigns
- Salesforce for Google AdWords

Setting up campaigns

Marketing is generally understood to be those activities which drive your organization's products and services. Sending marketing communications to your customers and prospects is important, but if it's a one-off mailing that you send and then forget, it might not be the most effective method of building your business. Using Salesforce's campaign feature allows you to create a series of communications, or a campaign, and track the results, including some basic ROI (return on investment) information.

Task A   Creating a campaign

The initial setup of a campaign requires some basic, but important information. What type of campaign are you creating? Direct mail, telemarketing, trade show, advertisement? What are your budgeted costs and expected response rates and revenue? Marketing efforts typically have costs associated with them, so setting up the campaign with the ROI or return on investment in mind on the front end is important.

To create a campaign:

1. Click on the Campaigns tab, or click the more arrow to the right of the last tab, and then click on Campaigns.
2. In the Recent Campaigns section, click New.
3. Assign a name to your campaign; select the Type from the drop-down.
4. In the Status drop-down, select the current status of the campaign, e.g., Planned, In Progress, Completed, Aborted.
5. Enter the Start and End dates for the campaign and click the Active check box to make the campaign active.
6. Enter a description if you like.
7. Enter the NumberSent, Expected Response, Expected Revenue, Budgeted Cost, and Actual Cost, if you know those figures.
8. Click Save.

Your Salesforce Administrator can edit the list of types of campaigns in the Setup | App Setup | Customize | Campaigns | Fields area. You can list the types of campaigns that your organization uses, such as trade show.

To view Campaigns, you'll need **Read** permission on **Campaigns**.

To create Campaigns, you'll need **Create** permission on **Campaigns** and Marketing User checked in your user information.

This feature is available in:

✔ Unlimited   ✔ Developer

✔ Enterprise   Group

$ Professional   Personal

Task B Adding tasks to a campaign

Planning the tasks involved in a campaign is an important step to the campaign's effectiveness. Will this be a single marketing effort like a large direct mail piece, or will it involve several communication steps, or touches, over time? That is sometimes referred to as drip marketing.

To add tasks to a campaign:

1. Click on the Campaigns tab, or click the more arrow to the right of the last tab, and then click on Campaigns.
2. Click on the name of the campaign to which you want to add tasks; this will take you to the Campaign Detail view.
3. In the Open Activities section, click New Task. To assign the task to a different user, click the Assigned To lookup icon to the right of the Assigned To field, and then select the user to whom to assign the task. Enter the Subject, Due Date, Priority, and Status. The activity is already linked to the campaign. You can associate the task with a particular contact or lead. You can indicate the Type of activity, Call, Meeting, or Other.
4. In the Additional Information section, select the medium for the activity from the drop-down choices of Email, Mail, or Phone.
5. In the Description Information section add any Comments.
6. If you like, click the Send Notification Email to send an email informing the user assigned to the task. The first time you select that check box, you will also be able to select a check box to Make this the default setting.
7. Click Save or Save & New Task to add other tasks to this campaign.

You can assign different tasks in the campaign to different Salesforce users, and Salesforce will kindly send the user an email with the information on his new assignment.

To view Campaigns, you'll need **Read** permission on **Campaigns**.

To create Campaigns, you'll need **Create** permission on **Campaigns** and Marketing User checked in your user information.

This feature is available in:

✔ Unlimited	✔ Developer
✔ Enterprise	Group
$ Professional	Personal

Task C — Adding events to a campaign

Events are a type of activity that is scheduled on the calendar. You can have multiple activities associated with a campaign. Some may be tasks that are not linked to the calendar; others may be events. For example, you might have several marketing activities related to an upcoming trade show, with the trade show as an event.

You can run an activity report in Salesforce that will give you information about upcoming activities and events.

To view Campaigns, you'll need **Read** permission on **Campaigns**.

To create Campaigns, you'll need **Create** permission on **Campaigns** and Marketing User checked in your user information.

To add events to a campaign:

1. Click on the Campaigns tab, or click the more arrow to the right of the last tab, and then click on Campaigns.
2. Click on the name of the campaign to which you want to add events; this will take you to the Campaign Detail view.
3. In the Open Activities section, click New Event. To assign the event to a different user, click the Assigned To lookup icon to the right of the Assigned To field, and then select the user to whom to assign the task. Enter the Subject, Location, and Date. Select the Time and Duration, or click the check box for All Day Event. Select the medium for the activity from the drop-down choices of Email, Mail, or Phone. Then select Type and Show Time As.
4. In the Description Information section add a description of the event.
5. In the Recurrence section you can click the check box to Create recurring series of events. Once you click the check box, you can set the Frequency, Start, and End dates for the recurrence.
6. If you like, click the Reminder check box to set a reminder for the event, and update the date and time for the reminder.
7. Click Save or Save & New Event to add other events to this campaign.

This feature is available in:

✔ Unlimited ✔ Developer
✔ Enterprise Group
$ Professional Personal

Task D Customizing member status for a campaign

When you are planning your marketing campaign, you need to think about and customize what Salesforce calls the member status. This is the categorization you will track for the recipients of your campaign. For an event, for example, you might want the following statuses: Sent, Responded, Attending, Declined. For a telemarketing campaign to get in front of your prospects, you might want the following: Call Attempted, Call Completed, Interested, Presentation Scheduled. Each campaign can have its own custom set of statuses.

To customize member status for a campaign:

1. Click on the Campaigns tab, or click the more arrow to the right of the last tab, and then click on Campaigns.
2. Click on the name of the campaign to which you want to add events; this will take you to the Campaign Detail view.
3. In the Campaign Detail section, click the Advanced Setup.
4. Click Edit to add, remove, or change any of the campaign member status options.
5. To add a status, click the Add More link and enter the status. To include a status in the Total Responses field on the campaign, click the Responded check box next to that status. You will need to choose one status as the default, by clicking the radio button next to that status. Click Save when you are done adding statuses.
6. Click Save when you are done adding statuses.

Tracking the response rate for a marketing campaign is pretty common, and you can use the custom member status feature to indicate which of the statuses constitutes a response. In the example of a marketing campaign for an event, you might consider both accepted invites and declined invites as responses.

To view Campaigns, you'll need **Read** permission on **Campaigns**.

To edit Campaigns, you'll need **Edit** permission on **Campaigns** and Marketing User checked in your user information.

Campaign Member Status
Client Conference

Help for this Page

Enter values for this picklist. Choose one value as the default status when the campaign member status is updated manually. Mark one or more values as "Responded" so that records with these status values are included in the # Responses statistic field.

Current Campaign	Client Conference		Status	Planned
Type	Seminar / Conference		Active	✓

Member Status	Responded *	Default *
Sent	☐	⦿
Responded	☑	○
Attending	☑	○
Declined	☑	○

Add More

Save Cancel

This feature is available in:

✔ Unlimited   ✔ Developer
✔ Enterprise   Group
$ Professional   Personal

Task E Adding members to a campaign

Targeting your campaign recipients is a critical part of any marketing campaign. You could design the best marketing communications in the world, but if it's not getting in front of the right customers and prospects, then it won't be very effective. There are a number of ways to add leads and contacts to a campaign; you can manually select existing leads and contacts or you can import a list of leads and add them to the campaign.

To add members to a campaign:

1. Click on the Campaigns tab, or click the more arrow to the right of the last tab, and then click on Campaigns.
2. Click on the name of the campaign to which you want to add campaign steps; this will take you to the Campaign Detail view.
3. In the Campaign Detail section, click the Manage Members button.
4. You can add Existing Contacts, Existing Leads, or you can Import a CSV file of new leads and add them to the campaign. For example, you could add a contact by clicking the Add Members – Existing Contacts link.
5. In Step 1, the campaign you selected above should be displayed, and you can set the Member Status to Sent or Responded and click Next.
6. From the list of contacts, click the check box next to each contact that you would like to add to the campaign. You can sort this list view and add additional columns to make it easier to select contacts. For more information on list views, see Chapter 5.
7. Click Add to Campaign and then click Done.

To view Campaigns, you'll need **Read** permission on **Campaigns**.

To edit Campaigns, you'll need **Edit** permission on **Campaigns** and Marketing User checked in your user information.

Campaign
Manage Members: Client Conference
Back to Campaign: Client Conference

Use this page to manage the members of this campaign. You can either add new members or update the campaign member status of existing members.

Mass Add Campaign Members

Add Members - Existing Contacts	Add existing contacts to this campaign all at once.
Add Members - Existing Leads	Add existing leads to this campaign all at once.
Add Members - Import File	Import a CSV file of new leads and associate them with this campaign. (Import Leads)

Mass Update the Status of Campaign Members

Update Status - Existing Contacts	Update the Status of existing contacts all at once.
Update Status - Existing Leads	Update the Status of existing leads all at once.
Update Status - Import File	Update lead or contact statuses from an imported CSV file. (Update Campaign History)

Tip: In addition to the tools on this page, you can use contact or lead reports to add or update up to 50,000 campaign members at a time.

This feature is available in:

✔ Unlimited	✔ Developer
✔ Enterprise	Group
$ Professional	Personal

Task F   Adding members to a campaign from a report

Reports are an excellent way to filter your existing leads and contacts and then add them to the appropriate campaign. You could run a report on all leads and contacts that meet a certain criteria, like interest in a specific product or geographic location, and then add all the leads and contacts that appear on that report to a campaign.

To add members to a campaign from a report:

1. Click on the Reports tab to go to the Reports Home page.
2. Run the report to find your target list of contacts, leads, or person accounts that you want to add to the campaign. We will use the Mailing List, in Tabular format, for this example.
3. When the report displays, click the Add to Campaign button, then click the Campaign Lookup icon to the right of the Campaign field and select the campaign.
4. Click Add Campaign.
5. Click the Campaign Lookup icon to the right of the Campaign field and select the campaign by clicking on the name of the campaign.
6. Set the Member Status to Sent or Responded, and select the radio button for whether or not to override the member status. This override selection will update the member status for all the contacts/leads in a report, so if you have manually updated the status of a contact, you will lose that update.
7. Click Add to Campaign and then click Done.

We cover reports in Chapter 11 of this book.

To view Campaigns, you'll need **Read** permission on **Campaigns**.

To create Campaigns, you'll need **Create** permission on **Campaigns** and Marketing User checked in your user information.

To run Reports, you'll need **Run Reports** and **Read** on the records in a report.

To add campaign members from a Report, you'll need **Edit** on Campaigns and **Read** on contacts and/or leads.

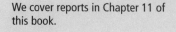

This feature is available in:

Task G   Cloning campaigns

Some campaigns are single events, while you might run other campaigns several times a year. If you are getting ready to launch a campaign that is similar to an existing campaign, you can save yourself time and typing by cloning that campaign.

To clone a campaign:

When cloning a campaign, be sure to give the new, cloned campaign a unique name. Salesforce will let you create a clone of the campaign with the exact same name, but it makes it hard to distinguish the campaigns from one another in the campaign list view if they have the same name.

Cloning a campaign will not clone the members, tasks ,or events, so you will have to add those elements to your newly cloned campaign. Also, when you clone a campaign, it is not marked as active, so you will need to check the active box as well.

To view Campaigns, you'll need **Read** permission on **Campaigns**.

To create Campaigns, you'll need **Create** permission on **Campaigns** and Marketing User checked in your user information.

To run Reports, you'll need **Run Reports** and **Read** on the records in a report.

To add campaign members from a Report, you'll need **Edit** on Campaigns and **Read** on contacts and/or leads.

1. Click on the Campaigns tab, or click the more arrow to the right of the last tab, and then click on Campaigns.
2. Click on the name of the campaign you want to clone; this will take you to the Campaign Detail view.
3. In the Campaign Detail section, click the Clone button.
4. In the Campaign Information section, edit the Campaign Name, Type, Status, Start, and End Dates and click the Active check box to make the campaign active.
5. You can now add members, tasks, and events to the new campaign.

This feature is available in:

✔ Unlimited	✔ Developer
✔ Enterprise	Group
$ Professional	Personal

Task H Finding campaigns

Mastering the search functionality is pretty critical in any sales tool, and Salesforce is no different. If you diligently enter all of your campaigns, then being able to quickly find a specific campaign when you need to update it is important. Luckily, the searching capabilities of Salesforce make it easy.

To find a campaign:

1. In the Search box in the sidebar on the left side of the Salesforce screen, click Campaigns from the drop-down.
2. Enter the search text, such as part of the campaign name, and click Go!
3. The list of campaigns that match that search will display and you can go to a specific campaign by clicking on the name of the campaign.

You can customize the list view of campaigns to view additional information about the campaign, like the Start Date, Type, Active, and more. For tips on customizing list views in Salesforce, see Chapter 5.

To view Campaigns, you'll need **Read** permission on **Campaigns**.

This feature is available in:

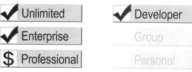

✔ Unlimited	✔ Developer
✔ Enterprise	Group
$ Professional	Personal

When you delete a campaign, all related tasks, events, and attachments are also deleted. The leads, contacts, and opportunities linked to that campaign are not deleted, but their relationship to that campaign is removed when you delete the campaign. Rather than deleting a campaign, you might want to consider simply deactivating the campaign by un-checking the Active check box in the campaign information section.

If you inadvertently deleted a campaign, you can retrieve that campaign from the Recycle Bin. Simply click on the Recycle Bin in the left sidebar, click the check box next to the campaign you want to recover, and click Undelete. This will restore the campaign, and all the other associated details, to your campaign list.

To delete Campaigns, you'll need **Delete** permission on **Campaigns** and Marketing User checked in your user information.

Task I Deleting campaigns

Over time you might need to clean up your list of campaigns, and some campaigns might be candidates for deletion. Deleting campaigns is very easy, provided you have the appropriate permission.

To delete a campaign:

1. Click on the Campaigns tab, or click the more arrow to the right of the last tab, and then click on Campaigns.
2. Click on the name of the campaign you want to delete; this will take you to the Campaign Detail view.
3. In the Campaign Detail section, click the Delete button.
4. Click OK in the Are you sure dialog box. You will be returned to the Campaign Home page.

This feature is available in:

✔ Unlimited ✔ Developer
✔ Enterprise Group
$ Professional Personal

Managing campaigns

Planning and executing a single campaign is great, but you might want to link several related campaigns together, and Salesforce provides a way to do that through campaign hierarchy. Just like an organizational hierarchy, a campaign hierarchy sets up the relationship between different campaigns.

Task A   Setting up campaign hierarchy

Linking related campaigns is a powerful tool that can assist in analyzing your campaign effectiveness. It also assists in grouping related marketing efforts so that you can easily see how they work together. For example, you might have a North American campaign. That campaign might have three child campaigns: USA, Canada, and Mexico.

To set up a campaign hierarchy:

1. Create the parent campaign. For steps in creating campaigns, see Section 1 of this chapter, Task A.
2. Create the associated campaigns for this parent campaign. Alternatively, if you created several campaigns before deciding to organize them in a hierarchy, edit the existing campaigns and associate them with the parent campaign.
3. You can select the parent campaign by clicking the lookup icon to the right of the Parent Campaign field, then clicking on the parent campaign name.
4. You will now be able to view, analyze, and report on all the related campaigns.

Your Salesforce Administrator will have to set up the campaign hierarchy function by adding the field for Parent Campaign to your campaign page layout.

Creating campaign hierarchies is another great opportunity for you and your team to sit back and do some thinking and planning for your marketing programs. Creating the overall parent campaign and then thinking through how the related campaigns fit together is an important step.

To create Campaigns, you'll need **Create** permission on **Campaigns** and Marketing User checked in your user information.

This feature is available in:

✔ Unlimited	✔ Developer
✔ Enterprise	Group
$ Professional	Personal

Task B   Viewing campaign hierarchy

Once you have set up your campaign hierarchy, you will be able to view the relationship between the campaigns, as well as some statistics for the entire hierarchy, such as total leads, total opportunities, value of opportunities, etc.

To view the campaign hierarchy:

1. Click on the Campaigns tab, or click the more arrow to the right of the last tab, and then click on Campaigns.
2. Click on the name of the campaign for which you want to view the hierarchy and click the View Hierarchy link next to the campaign name.
3. The campaign hierarchy will be displayed, showing the campaign you selected in bold.
4. You can view the details of any campaign in the hierarchy by clicking the campaign name.

You can customize the campaign list view to display some of the statistics for the hierarchy, like total Contacts and Leads. Customizing your list views is covered in Chapter 5 of this book.

To view Campaigns, you'll need **Read** permission on **Campaigns** and Marketing User checked in your user information.

Campaign Name	Campaign Type	Campaign Status	Active	Campaign Owner
Client Conference	Seminar / Conference	Planned	✓	Max Roach
Product Launch	Public Relations	Planned	✓	Max Roach

The hierarchy is created by associating campaigns with parent campaigns.

This feature is available in:

✔ Unlimited	✔ Developer
✔ Enterprise	Group
$ Professional	Personal

Task C   Mass updating campaigns

Once you have planned your campaign, targeted your campaign members, and then executed on the campaign, the real fun begins—tracking the effectiveness of that campaign. You can update the status of your campaign members one by one, or en masse—a whole bunch all at once.

To mass update a campaign:

1. Click on the Campaigns tab, or click the more arrow to the right of the last tab, and then click on Campaigns.
2. Click on the name of the campaign you want to update.
3. In the Campaign Detail section, click the Manage Members button.
4. Under the Mass Update the Status of Campaign Members section, click the Update Status – Existing Contacts link.
5. Select the Member Status, such as Responded, from the drop-down and click Next.
6. Click the check box for all the contacts that have responded, and then when you are finished, click Update Statuses and then click Done.

If your responses are collected outside of Salesforce, you can import those responses and mass update the member status through that import process. You can only import up to 3,000 existing leads or contacts at one time, however.

For more details on mass updating campaign member status, click on the Help for this Page link in the top-right corner of the Manage Members screen.

To update Campaigns, you'll need **Read** permission on **Campaigns** and **Read** on all contacts, leads, and accounts, and Marketing User checked in your user information.

This feature is available in:

✔ Unlimited   ✔ Developer

✔ Enterprise   Group

$ Professional   Personal

Task D   Updating campaigns by contacts

Some campaigns, like telemarketing programs, require touching each campaign lead or contact one by one. You can update a lead or contact on an individual basis for these cases.

To update Campaigns for a contact, you'll need **Read** permission on **Campaigns** and **Edit** on related contacts, leads, and accounts.

To update a campaign for a contact:

1. Click on the Contacts tab to go to the Contacts Home page, or search for a contact using the search box on the sidebar on the left side of the screen.
2. Select the contact by clicking on the contact name.
3. In the Campaign History section, click the Edit button.
4. Select the campaign from the drop-down and click Next.
5. Select the status from the drop-down, e.g., Responded, and click Save.

This feature is available in:

✔ Unlimited   ✔ Developer
✔ Enterprise   Group
$ Professional   Personal

Task E — Associating an opportunity with a campaign

The bottom line for any campaign is how effective it was. Measuring the campaign effectiveness depends on how you want to calculate your ROI, or return on investment. For most organizations, sales opportunities that result in closed deals and revenue are pretty clear returns on the marketing dollars spent. To calculate that ROI, you will need to associate your opportunities with the appropriate campaign.

To associate an opportunity with a campaign:

1. If you are in the Campaign Detail view, in the Opportunities section, click New. Or you can click on the Opportunities tab to go to the Opportunities Home page and select an opportunity by clicking on the opportunity name.
2. If you are creating a new opportunity, enter all of the opportunity information; if you are editing an existing opportunity, in the Opportunity Detail section, click Edit.
3. Click the lookup icon to the right of the Campaign Source field.
4. Search for the campaign, and click on the name of the campaign.
5. Click Save. Now you can click on the campaign source in the Opportunity Detail section and the opportunity will be reflected in the campaign statistics.

Your administrator will have to add the Campaign Source field to your opportunity page layout in order for you to be able to associate opportunities with campaigns.

To update Campaigns for a contact, you'll need **Read** permission on **Campaigns** and **Edit** on related contacts, leads, and accounts.

This feature is available in:

✔ Unlimited   ✔ Developer
✔ Enterprise   Group
$ Professional   Personal

Task F   Updating campaign status

Campaigns, like opportunities, have defined stages that will help you manage your campaigns more effectively. You can set the status of a campaign to Planned, In Progress, Completed, or Aborted.

To update the campaign status:

1. Click on the Campaigns tab, or click the more arrow to the right of the last tab, and then click on Campaigns.
2. Click on the name of the campaign you want to update.
3. In the Campaign Detail section, click Edit.
4. Change the Status to In Progress, Completed, or Aborted and click Save.

Your Salesforce Administrator can customize the campaign status options for your organization. This is done in Setup | App Setup | Customize | Fields. One status you might want to add is Suspended, for campaigns that are ongoing but may be temporarily on hold due to other issues in your organization or your industry.

To view Campaigns, you'll need **Read** permission on **Campaigns**.

To edit Campaigns, you'll need **Edit** permission on **Campaigns** and Marketing User checked in your user information.

This feature is available in:

✔ Unlimited	✔ Developer
✔ Enterprise	Group
$ Professional	Personal

Task G Viewing campaign statistics

Tracking how effective a particular campaign is for your organization is very important, and Salesforce provides an easy way to view the relevant statistics for a particular campaign.

To view campaign statistics:

1. Click on the Campaigns tab, or click the more arrow to the right of the last tab, and then click on Campaigns.
2. Click on the name of the campaign for which you want to view current statistics.
3. In the Campaign Detail section, click the Other Information section to display the statistics.
4. You can now view statistics for the campaign, such as total responses, leads, converted leads, etc.

Keeping tabs of the statistics for an individual campaign allows you to make more effective marketing decisions during the campaign. You can evaluate the results to date, and then make changes to the remainder of the campaign based on your analysis of those results.

To view Campaigns, you'll need **Read** permission on **Campaigns**.

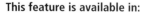

This feature is available in:

Task H   Running campaign reports

On the Campaign Home tab there is a section for reports, with three standard campaign reports that you can run with just a few clicks. Reports can be filtered, sorted, customized, saved, and exported to Excel. Reports are a key tool in evaluating the success of your campaigns.

To run a campaign report:

1. Click on the Campaigns tab, or click the more arrow to the right of the last tab, and then click on Campaigns.

2. In the Reports section, click the report you want to run, such as Campaign ROI analysis report.

3. In the Report Options section, choose if you want the report data summarized, and which campaigns you want to view in the report, e.g., All campaigns, All active campaigns, My campaigns, etc. Or to run the report for a specific campaign, from the View pull-down, choose Select a campaign, and then click the lookup icon to the right of the Select campaign field and select a campaign name and click Run Report.

4. You can now save, print, or export this report.

See Chapter 11 of this book for more information on Reports as well as detailed steps on filtering, sorting, customizing, and exporting reports to Excel.

There are only three reports on the Campaign home tab, but in the Reports home tab there are seven reports for campaigns, so if you are not seeing the reports you want, just click on the Reports tab and then scroll down to the section with the campaign reports.

To view Campaigns, you'll need **Read** permission on **Campaigns**.

To run Reports, you'll need **Run Reports** permission and **Read** permission on the records included in the report.

This feature is available in:

✔ Unlimited	✔ Developer
✔ Enterprise	Group
$ Professional	Personal

Salesforce for Google AdWords

Chances are that your marketing programs include some sort of Internet marketing strategy. If you are not using Google AdWords as part of that strategy, then you might want to consider adding this powerful tool to your bag of lead-generation tricks. Google AdWords is an online service, also known as pay-per-click. Your organization pays Google to display your company's information based on keywords that prospects search on using Google. Salesforce for Google AdWords links this powerful Internet-marketing tool with your database, which allows you to track the effectiveness of your Google AdWord campaigns right in Salesforce.

Task A   Setting up a Google AdWords account

The process to set up Google AdWords has three steps:

1. Set up a Google AdWords account.
2. Set up your website to track leads from Google AdWords.
3. Track the leads in Salesforce that result from your Google AdWords. In Salesforce, you can either set up a new Google AdWord account, or if you already have an account, you can link that account to Salesforce.

To set up a Google AdWords account:

1. In Salesforce, click the more button to the left of the tabs and then click the Google AdWords Setup.
2. Enter your Email, create a Password, determine your Currency and Time Zone, and click Create New Account.
3. Alternatively, if you already have a Google AdWords account, simply enter your customer ID and click Link Account.
4. Salesforce will then process your request, after which you can log into Google AdWords and set up your AdWords.

If you are already using Google AdWords and have an existing account, you can enter your AdWords Customer ID and link your AdWords account to Salesforce.

Effectively using this powerful Internet-advertising tool is part art, part science. For more details and hints on configuring Google AdWords, you can log into your Google AdWords account and view more information at https://adwords.google.com/support/.

This feature is available in:

✔ Unlimited	✔ Developer
✔ Enterprise	✔ Group
✔ Professional	Personal

On the Google AdWords home tab in Salesforce, there is a section for Frequently Asked Questions with links to documents that will help you through the setup process.

Task B   Setting up your website to track leads from Google AdWords

Setting up a Google AdWords account is just the first step; now you need to configure your website to receive and track those leads. Depending on your organization, you might need to enlist the help of whoever manages your company's website. You basically want to direct those leads that found your company through Google to a specific page in your website when they click on your link.

To set up your website to track leads from Google AdWords:

1. In Salesforce, click the more button to the left of the tabs and then click the Google AdWords Setup.
2. In the AdWords Lead Tracking section, click Set up Lead Tracking.
3. In Step 1, click Create Web-to-Lead Form.
4. Select the fields to be included on your web form, then enter a URL landing page that your leads will be taken to once they fill out the form. It can be the home page of your website, or you can use a page that thanks them for submitting their information.
5. Select the language for the form, either Default or English.
6. Change the order of the fields by clicking on the field and clicking the up or down button.
7. Click Generate. Salesforce will create the HTML for your web form, which you can copy and paste into a document or email for your web designer, or you can update your website with this form. Click in the box with the sample HTML and select all the text by clicking Ctrl + A. Copy by clicking Crtl + C, open an email or Notepad file, and paste the HTML by clicking Crtl + V.
8. In Step 2 you will add tracking codes to your website. Click View Instructions. You can either copy this code and paste it into an email to your web designer or you can click the Email to webmaster link in Step 2.
9. In Step 3 you can test your website to make sure that the web form and tracking codes are set up properly to capture the lead tracking information. Click Test Your Setup, and enter the URL of the pages of your website where you added the Salesforce tracking codes. For the page that also has the web form, click the Web-to-Lead Form check box as well. To add additional pages to the test, click the Add More URLs link and then click Run Test. If there are any issues, Salesforce will identify them and you can address those and re-run the test. Once the pages are setup correctly, you can click Finished.
10. Click Done.

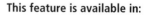

This feature is available in:

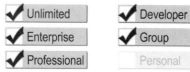

Unlimited   Developer

Enterprise   Group

Professional   Personal

Task C Viewing leads in Salesforce for Google AdWords

Once you have set up the Google AdWords account and configured your website to track those click-throughs from Google, you can now view your resulting leads in Salesforce. There are four places where you can view lead information related to Google AdWords: the Google AdWords Account Summary, Lead Source Details, Reports, and Dashboards.

To view leads in Salesforce for Google AdWords:

1. Google AdWords Setup tab—In Salesforce, click the more button to the left of the tabs and then click the Google AdWords Setup. In the Account Summary section, you can view the status of leads generated by source, including Google AdWords, Organic Search, Web Referral, or Web Direct.

2. Leads—To view the lead source, click the Leads tab and then view your leads with the lead source information. Salesforce also creates an activity record for each lead with the information about the lead source. For leads generated by your Google AdWords, this activity record includes the AdWords campaign, ad group, keyword, text ad, search term, and the referring URL.

3. Reports—Salesforce has 20 reports specifically for Google AdWords. Click the Reports tab and from the Folder drop-down, select Google AdWord Reports, and then click on the report name to view the report.

4. Dashboards—In the Google AdWords Setup tab, you can also view the data in a dashboard format. In the AdWords Lead Tracking section, click the Google AdWords Dashboard link in the lower-right corner. You can then view the number of leads generated, Top AdWord Performers, and Opportunity Pipeline information in a graphical form.

Organic leads are those where the prospect, or lead, has run a search on a major search engine and clicked on your website in the search results, but not on a paid link, like Google AdWords. At the time of this book printing, Salesforce tracked clicks from these major search engines: Google, Yahoo!, MSN, Altavista, AOL, A9, Ask.com, Lycos, Mamma, Netscape, and EarthLink.

To view Leads, Dashboards and Reports, you'll need **Read** permission on **Leads, Dashboards** and **Reports**.

To run Reports, you'll need **Run Reports** permission and **Read** permission on the records included in the report.

Reports
Google AdWords Reports

Printable View | Help for this Page

Folder Google AdWords Reports   ▼   Edit | Create New Folder

A | B | C | D | E | F | G | H | I | J | K | L | M | N | O | P | Q | R | S | T | U | V | W | X | Y | Z | Other All

Create New Custom Report

Action	Report Name ^	Description	Last Modified By	Last Modified Date
Edit | Del | Export	Ad Group Lead Report	Show all Leads from Google AdWords, organized by Ad Group	Roach, Max	3/15/2008 2:29 PM
Edit | Del | Export	Ad Group Pipeline Report	Show all Opportunities from Google AdWords, organized by Ad Group	Roach, Max	3/15/2008 2:29 PM
Edit | Del | Export	Ad Group Revenue Report	Show all closed Opportunities and revenue, organized by Ad Group	Roach, Max	3/15/2008 2:29 PM
Edit | Del | Export	Google Campaign Lead Report	Show all Leads from Google AdWords, organized by Google Campaign	Roach, Max	3/15/2008 2:29 PM
Edit | Del | Export	Google Campaign Leads by Date	Show all Leads from Google AdWords over time	Roach, Max	3/15/2008 2:29 PM
Edit | Del | Export	Google Campaign Pipeline by Date	Show all pipeline generated from Google AdWords over time	Roach, Max	3/15/2008 2:29 PM
Edit | Del | Export	Google Campaign Pipeline by Stage	Show the Opportunites by stage from Google AdWords	Roach, Max	3/15/2008 2:29 PM
Edit | Del | Export	Google Campaign Pipeline Report	Show all Opportunities from Google AdWords, organized by Google Campaign	Roach, Max	3/15/2008 2:29 PM
Edit | Del | Export	Google Campaign Revenue Report	Show all closed Opportunities and revenue, organized by Google Campaign	Roach, Max	3/15/2008 2:29 PM
Edit | Del | Export	Keyword Lead Report	Show all Leads from Google AdWords, organized by Keyword	Roach, Max	3/15/2008 2:29 PM
Edit | Del | Export	Keyword Pipeline Report	Show all Opportunities from Google AdWords, organized by Keyword	Roach, Max	3/15/2008 2:29 PM
Edit | Del | Export	Keyword Revenue Report	Show all closed Opportunities and revenue, organized by Keyword	Roach, Max	3/15/2008 2:29 PM
Edit | Del | Export	Search Phrase Lead Report	Show all Leads from organic and paid search, organized by Search Phrase	Roach, Max	3/15/2008 2:29 PM
Edit | Del | Export	Search Phrase Pipeline Report	Show all Opportunities from organic and paid search, organized by Search Phrase	Roach, Max	3/15/2008 2:29 PM
Edit | Del | Export	Search Phrase Revenue Report	Show all closed Opportunities and revenue, organized by Search Phrase	Roach, Max	3/15/2008 2:29 PM
Edit | Del | Export	Text Ad Lead Report	Show all Leads from Google AdWords, organized by Text Ad	Roach, Max	3/15/2008 2:29 PM
Edit | Del | Export	Text Ad Pipeline Report	Show all Opportunities from Google AdWords, organized by Text Ad	Roach, Max	3/15/2008 2:29 PM
Edit | Del | Export	Text Ad Revenue Report	Show all closed Opportunities and revenue, organized by Text Ad	Roach, Max	3/15/2008 2:29 PM
Edit | Del | Export	Web Lead Source	Leads Organized by Website Lead Source	Roach, Max	3/15/2008 2:29 PM
Edit | Del | Export	Web Lead Source by Date	Trend of Web Leads by Website Lead Source	Roach, Max	3/15/2008 2:29 PM

Show me fewer ▲ records per list page

This feature is available in:

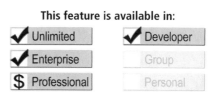

✔ Unlimited   ✔ Developer
✔ Enterprise   Group
$ Professional   Personal

Task D   Disconnecting your Google AdWords account from Salesforce

You might not always want to link Salesforce with your Google AdWords account, so in the event that you want to disconnect the two, you will have to log into both applications.

To disconnect your Google AdWords account from Salesforce:

1. In Salesforce, click the more button to the left of the tabs and then click the Google AdWords Setup.
2. In the AdWords Account Link section, click Change.
3. Log into your Google AdWords account at www.google.com/adwords.
4. Click the My Account tab, and then click on the Access link.
5. In the Client Managers section, you should see salesforce.mcc@salesforce.com. Click the Terminate Access link and click OK.
6. In Salesforce, the Google AdWords Setup tab will default back to the setup page, so you can re-link your Google AdWords account for a new campaign in the future.

Google
AdWords

| Campaign Management | Reports | Analytics | **My Account** |

Billing Summary | Billing Preferences | Access | Account Preferences

Access to this AdWords Account
If you manage this AdWords account with others, see who has access to sign in. Invite others to create their own login email and password to access this account by clicking 'Invite other users.' Learn more

+ Invite other users

	AdWords User	Access Level	
Users With Account Access	info@po3inc.com Last logged in Mar 19, 2008 ⑦	Administrative Access ⑦	You cannot change or terminate your own access to AdWords.
Client Managers	salesforce.mcc@salesforce.com adwords.mcc@kieden.com	API only	Terminate access

Microsoft Internet Explorer   ☒

? Are you sure you wish to remove manager access to this account?

OK   Cancel

This feature is available in:

✔ Unlimited   ✔ Developer
✔ Enterprise   ✔ Group
✔ Professional   Personal

Chapter 11

Reports & Dashboards

- Reports
- Dashboards

Reports

Reports are a great tool to help you manage your business. Reports, unlike views within a database, can be printed and shared with anyone at your organization, even people that are not users in your Salesforce database. Salesforce has over 50 reports to help you analyze and view the status of your leads, accounts, contacts, opportunities, forecasts, campaigns, activities, and more. And customizing the reports is simple and straightforward, so you can run the reports that will provide you with relevant data.

Task A   Running a report

You probably have a great deal of valuable data in your Salesforce database. Reports allow you to view and filter that data to assist you in analyzing your business and making more informed decisions.

To run a report:

1. Click on the Reports tab.
2. The All Reports tab shows every report you can access, and the Recent Reports tab shows the list of reports that you have run recently.
3. Select a report by clicking on the name of the report.
4. If you have the Unlimited, Enterprise, Developer, or Professional versions, there will be a Report Folders section, and you can click the drop-down to view a specific type of report, e.g., Sales Reports. You will then be viewing a list of the reports, with a short description of each report.
5. The report will display, and you can now sort, filter, customize, print, or export the results.

All editions of Salesforce include reports, but the specific reports that are available to you depend on your edition of Salesforce.

To run Reports, you'll need **Run Reports** permission and **Read** permission on the records included in reports.

To create, save, and delete Reports, you'll need **Run Reports** permission, **Create and Customize Reports**, as well as **Read** permission on the records included in reports.

This feature is available in:

✔ Unlimited	✔ Developer
✔ Enterprise	✔ Group
✔ Professional	✔ Personal

Task B   Printing reports

After running your report, you can quickly jump to a printable view that will open Microsoft Excel, where you can format and print your report.

To print a report:

1. Click on the Reports tab, or click the more arrow and click Reports.
2. The All Reports tab shows every report you can access, and the Recent Reports tab shows the list of reports that you have run recently.
3. Select a report by clicking on the name of the report.
4. Click the Printable View button and Open; this will display the report in an Excel format.
5. From the File drop-down, select Print; select your printer and click OK.

> To run Reports, you'll need **Run Reports** permission and **Read** permission on the records included in reports.

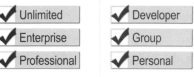

This feature is available in:

✔ Unlimited	✔ Developer
✔ Enterprise	✔ Group
✔ Professional	✔ Personal

Task C   Saving a report with filters

If you find yourself running the same report, and entering the same filter criteria, you might want to consider saving that report to save time. The next time you want to run that report, you can run your saved version and you won't have to re-enter your filters and criteria.

If you have role hierarchies in your organization (e.g., VP Sales, Sales Managers, Sales Representatives, etc.), when you save a report, you can click the Save Hierarchy Level check box. This will only allow users at your same hierarchy level or above to see this saved report.

To run Reports, you'll need **Run Reports** permission and **Read** permission on the records included in reports.

To save Reports, you'll need **Create and Customize Reports** permission.

To save Reports to a specific public folder, you'll need **Manage Public Reports** permission.

To save a report with filters:

1. Click on the Reports tab, or click the more arrow and click Reports.
2. The All Reports tab shows every report you can access, and the Recent Reports tab shows the list of reports that you have run recently.
3. Select a report by clicking on the name of the report. For this example we will use the Mailing List report. Select the Tabular Report radio button and click Run Report.
4. Select the report filters you want to apply. For more information on filtering reports, see Task D in the Reports section of this chapter.
5. Sort the report. For more information on sorting reports, see Task E in the Reports section of this chapter.
6. Click the Save As button.
7. Give your report a name and enter a description. If you are an administrator, or you have Manage Public Reports permission enabled, you can select the report folder in which to save the report. The default folder is My Personal Custom Reports.
8. Click Save or Save & Return to Report.

This feature is available in:

Task D Saving a report from the printable Excel view

Once you have run your report, you can open the printable view in Excel, and you can then save the report to the location of your choice.

To save a report from the printable Excel view:

1. Click on the Reports tab, or click the more arrow and click Reports.
2. The All Reports tab shows every report you can access, and the Recent Reports tab shows the list of reports that you have run recently.
3. Select a report by clicking on the name of the report.
4. Click the Printable View button and Open; this will display the report in an Excel format.
5. From the File drop-down, select Save As.
6. In the Save in drop-down at the top of the Save As dialog box, choose the location where you would like to save this report. In the File name field, change the name of the file, if you like. In the Save as type field, change the type to Microsoft Office Excel Workbook (*.xls).
7. Click Save and the click File | Exit to close Excel.

Once reports are saved, they are not updated. They're a snapshot in time. If you add new data to Salesforce, you'll have to re-run the report to include this new information in the analysis.

To run Reports, you'll need **Run Reports** permission and **Read** permission on the records included in reports.

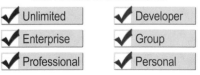

This feature is available in:

✔ Unlimited	✔ Developer
✔ Enterprise	✔ Group
✔ Professional	✔ Personal

Task E   Filtering reports

For reports to be effective management and analysis tools, you need to be able to quickly and easily adjust the data in the report to match your current information need. Salesforce provides powerful mechanisms to filter reports so that you can view and drill down on just the data you need, when you need it.

To filter a report:

1. Click on the Reports tab, or click the more arrow and click Reports.
2. The All Reports tab shows every report you can access, and the Recent Reports tab shows the list of reports that you have run recently.
3. Select a report by clicking on the name of the report. For this example we will use the Mailing List report. Select the Tabular Report radio button and click Run Report.
4. At the top of the screen, click the Summarize information by drop-down and choose a field in the report to summarize on, such as Contact Owner or Mailing State/Province.
5. Click the View drop-down and select All Accounts.
6. In the Time Frame area, click the Columns drop-down and select the field you want to use to filter on, such as Created Date. In the duration drop-down, you can select one of the predefined durations, such as Current CY (Calendar Year), or you can select Custom and then enter a Start and End Date for your time frame.
7. Click Run Report; now the report will run with the filters you have applied.
8. If your report selection has further filter and drill-down options, there will be check boxes next to the sections; click a check box to further filter the report by those report elements.
9. If you want to drill down on a particular field, scroll to the bottom of the report and in the drill down by field, select a field to use, such as Mailing City, and click Drill Down.

For more help on using filters and criteria, click on the Help for this Page link in the top-right corner of the Reports Home tab.

To run Reports, you'll need **Run Reports** permission and **Read** permission on the records included in reports.

This feature is available in:

✔ Unlimited	✔ Developer
✔ Enterprise	✔ Group
✔ Professional	✔ Personal

Task F   Sorting reports

Salesforce provides the ability to quickly re-sort a report based on any of the column headers, or data elements, in a report. Sorting your report can really save a lot of time. For example, if you have a report that includes a currency field, sorting by this currency field will show all of your high dollar amount records near the top of the report.

To sort a report:

1. Click on the Reports tab, or click the more arrow and click Reports.
2. The All Reports tab shows every report you can access, and the Recent Reports tab shows the list of reports that you have run recently.
3. Select a report by clicking on the name of the report. For this example we will use the Mailing List report. Select the Tabular Report radio button and click Run Report.
4. Select the report filters you want to apply. For more information on filtering reports, see Task D in the Reports section of this chapter.
5. To sort the report by one of the column headers, click on the name of the column.
6. The report will now be sorted in ascending order by that column, and a small triangle will appear in the column header, pointing up.
7. To sort descending, simply click the column header again.

To run Reports, you'll need **Run Reports** permission and **Read** permission on the records included in reports.

This feature is available in:

✔ Unlimited	✔ Developer
✔ Enterprise	✔ Group
✔ Professional	✔ Personal

Task G　Setting up Excel integration

If you are like most organizations, you are probably using one or more Microsoft Excel spreadsheets to help in analyzing and managing your business. One of the nice features of Salesforce reports is the ability to integrate directly with Excel. To use this powerful functionality, you'll need to install the integration between Excel and Salesforce. It's a fairly straightforward process, called Force.com Connect for Microsoft Office, and it includes an add-in for both Word and Excel. The Word integration is handy when it comes to producing template-based documents from Salesforce.

To set up Excel integration:

For more information on Security Tokens, see Chapter 16 of this book.

To install the Connect for Office Integration, you might need to log into your computer with a user profile that has Administrative privileges.

1. On your local machine, close all open programs; specifically, you will need to close all Microsoft Office applications, including Word, Excel, and Outlook.
2. In Salesforce, click Setup; then under the Personal Setup section in the sidebar on the left, click Desktop Integration.
3. Click Connect for Microsoft Office.
4. Click Install Now or Yes.
5. You will now be in the installer wizard; click Next.
6. Click the I accept radio button and click Next.
7. Click Finish. You will have to restart your computer for the Connect for Office integration to be complete. Click Yes to restart immediately, or No to restart later.
8. When you open Excel, you should now see a Salesforce.com drop-down on the toolbar.

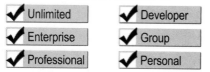

This feature is available in:

✔ Unlimited	✔ Developer
✔ Enterprise	✔ Group
✔ Professional	✔ Personal

Task H Importing Salesforce reports to Microsoft Excel

You can import Salesforce reports directly into Excel and then do further analysis of your Salesforce data. Also, once you have the data in Excel, you can print, save, and email that spreadsheet.

To import Salesforce reports to Microsoft Excel:

1. Open Microsoft Excel and click on the Salesforce.com drop-down on the toolbar and select Log in. You will need to enter your username and password, with your security token. For information on setting up and using security tokens for the Microsoft Office integration, see Chapter 16 in this book.
2. Click on the Salesforce.com drop-down on the toolbar and select Import a Report.
3. The Get a Report dialog box will display with a list of the Salesforce reports. Click on a report to select.
4. In the Destination worksheet you can enter a name for your report.
5. In the Cell field, you can enter the specific cell in your Excel worksheet where you want to place the data.
6. Choose either the Raw Data or Formatted radio button. Raw data imports the data without any totals. The Formatted option preserves the colors, fonts, subtotals, and totals from the Salesforce report.
7. You can now work with the report in Excel and print or save the Excel worksheet.

Before you can import reports into Microsoft Excel, you will need to set up the Connect for Microsoft Office. See Task F in the Reports section of this chapter.

To import reports in Excel, you'll need **Run Reports** and **Export Reports** permission and **Read** permission on the records included in reports.

This feature is available in:

✔ Unlimited   ✔ Developer
✔ Enterprise   ✔ Group
✔ Professional   ✔ Personal

Task I Refreshing Salesforce data in Excel reports

Once you import data and save it in Excel, the data is only as updated as your last import or refresh. Any new data added to Salesforce will not appear in the Excel spreadsheet, but after a simple refresh process, the data in Excel can be automatically replaced with the most current data from Salesforce.

To refresh Salesforce data in Excel reports:

1. In Microsoft Excel, open the report you would like to refresh from the location where you saved it. To import a report into Excel, see Task G in the Reports section of this report.

2. Click on the Salesforce.com drop-down on the Excel toolbar and select either Refresh Selected or Refresh All. Refresh All will refresh all of the reports you have previously imported into Excel.

3. If you chose Refresh Selected you will be viewing a list of the reports you had imported to Excel and saved. Select a report by clicking on the name of the report and then click Refresh Selected.

4. If your report contained pivot tables, and you want to also refresh those pivot tables, click the Update Pivot Tables check box. Click Refresh Selected.

5. You will now be viewing the report you opened, with the latest data from Salesforce included.

Try not to rename the Excel files that contain imported reports from Salesforce, because when you rename a file, the connection between that Excel file and Salesforce is lost, and you will not be able to refresh the report. You would then have to re-import the report into Excel and re-save it.

To refresh reports in Excel, you'll need **Run Reports** and **Export Reports** permission and **Read** permission on the records included in reports.

This feature is available in:

- ✔ Unlimited
- ✔ Enterprise
- ✔ Professional
- ✔ Developer
- ✔ Group
- ✔ Personal

Task J   Customizing a standard report

Chances are good that you'll need a custom report at some point. The standard reports in Salesforce will give you a good idea of what can be done with the reporting feature, but the real power of the reports aren't realized until you customize the reports.

To customize a standard report:

1. Click on the Reports tab, or click the more arrow and click Reports.

2. The All Reports tab shows every report you can access, and the Recent Reports tab shows the list of reports that you have run recently.

3. Select a report by clicking on the name of the report. For this example we will use the Closed Opportunities report.

4. Click the Customize button.

5. In Step 2, select the columns you would like to include in your report by clicking the check box next to the field name, or to remove a column from a report, clear the check box for that field. When you are done adding/removing columns, click Next in the lower-right corner of the screen.

6. In Step 3, you can select the columns that you want to sum or average by clicking the appropriate check box. You can also choose to select the Largest or Smallest Value, and then click Next.

7. In Step 4, you can reorder the columns. Simply click a column and then click the Up or Down button. You can also select the Top or Bottom button to make a column the first or last column in your report.

8. In Step 5, you can set the Standard Filters for the report. You can also set Advanced filters. In the Limit Row count, you can set the report to display a limited amount of data. For example, in a Closed Opportunities report you can limit the row maximum to 10 and in the Sort by drop-down, select Amount, and set the Order radio button to Descending. Your report will only include the top 10 largest deals closed.

9. Click Run Report and view the report with your customization changes. You can click Customize to make any additional changes to the report.

10. Click Save As and enter a Report Name, Description, and if you are an administrator, or you have the Manage Public Reports permission enabled, you can select the report folder in which to save the report. The default folder is My Personal Custom Reports. Click Save or Save & Return to Report.

To run Reports, you'll need **Run Reports** permission and **Read** permission on the records included in reports.

To create, edit, save, and delete Reports, you'll need **Create and Customize Reports** permission.

This feature is available in:

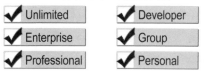

✔ Unlimited	✔ Developer
✔ Enterprise	✔ Group
✔ Professional	✔ Personal

Dashboards

Salesforce has a very powerful and functional tool that displays the most important information in your database—the dashboard. The dashboard in your car is designed to give you up-to-the-minute information that will help you drive; the dashboards in Salesforce provide the same kind of immediate view into important elements that you can use to better manage your business. The Dashboard view is also easily customized and filtered to select only the most relevant data specific to your business model and/or sales process.

Task A   Viewing dashboards

Dashboards are designed to display the most critical data and information in your database, and present that data in a way that facilitates quick evaluation of the key indicators for your business. Want to see the current Opportunity Pipeline as well as track the status of new leads? Just go to the Dashboards view in Salesforce.

To view dashboards:

1. Click on the Dashboards tab, or click the more arrow and click Dashboards.
2. In the Dashboard Home view, click the View Dashboard drop-down to select a particular dashboard view.
3. In the top-right corner of the Dashboard, there is an As of date and time field. To refresh the data in a dashboard, click the refresh button.
4. To view a list of Dashboards, click the Go to Dashboard List link on the top-left corner of the Dashboard view. From the dashboard list, click in the Folder drop-down to select a dashboard folder and then click on the name of the dashboard to view it.

When you click on the Dashboard tab, Salesforce displays the dashboard you last viewed.

Dashboards do a good job of summarizing report data. A report might show you a long list of all of the sales in a specific territory. A dashboard might display the same data in the form of a pie chart or bar graph.

To view Dashboards, you'll need **Run Reports** and **Manage Dashboard** permissions.

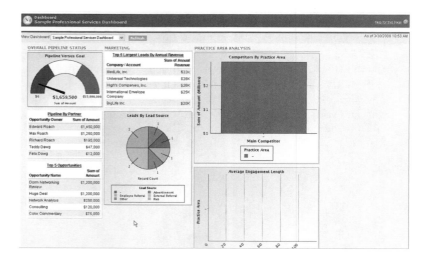

This feature is available in:

- ✔ Unlimited
- ✔ Enterprise
- ✔ Professional
- ✔ Developer
- Group
- Personal

Task B Creating a dashboard

The default dashboard views in Salesforce are very good, but you can create dashboards and customize the data you display to more closely map to your business model and/or sales process. You can quickly and easily add and remove components from a dashboard, as well as change the way the data is displayed. And if you have customized any reports, you can build dashboards that will graphically represent the data in those custom reports.

To create a dashboard:

1. The first step in creating a dashboard is to create the custom report that includes the information you want to see in your dashboard. The steps to customize a standard report are in Task J in the Reports section of this chapter.

2. Once you have customized your report, click on the Dashboards tab, or click the more arrow and click Dashboards.

3. Click Go to Dashboard List link on the top-left corner of the Dashboard view and click New Dashboard button.

4. In the Dashboard settings section, give your dashboard a title and enter a description if you like. Select the Dashboard Layout Style from the drop-down.

5. In the Dashboard Security Settings section, click the lookup icon to the right of the Running User field. Select the user that has the security settings you want to apply to your dashboard. If you want all sales representatives to view the dashboard, then select a user that is a sales representative. You will need to have View All Data permission to select a user other than yourself. Select a Folder from the drop-down to save your custom dashboard to a specific folder. The default is the Sample Dashboards folder.

6. In the Default Chart Settings you can control the look and feel of the dashboard. You can set colors and text size. Click Save.

7. For each of the columns you created, you will now need to add components. Click Add Component under the first column.

8. In Step 1, Component Setting, choose the radio button for the type of dashboard graphic you would like, Chart, Table, Metric, Gauge, or a Custom S-Control. Enter the header and footer text you want on your dashboard, if any. Give your dashboard a title. You can select the Display Units to display in millions, billions, etc.

9. In Step 2, Source report, click the Custom Report drop-down to select your custom report.

To create and edit Dashboards, you'll need **Manage Dashboards** permission.

This feature is available in:

✔ Unlimited	✔ Developer
✔ Enterprise	Group
✔ Professional	Personal

10. In Step 3, Chart Settings, choose the Chart Type, and set whether the chart will sort ascending or descending and by label or value in the Sort By drop-down. Select the Maximum Value to display and the legend position. If you want to set the Axis Range, select Manual from the Axis Range drop-down and then enter the Range Minimum and Maximum. Click Save. Repeat this step for each column in your dashboard; then click Done.

11. You can now select your custom dashboard from the Dashboard List.

This feature is available in:

✔ Unlimited	✔ Developer
✔ Enterprise	Group
✔ Professional	Personal

Task C   Cloning a dashboard

Once you start working with dashboards in Salesforce, you will quickly realize how effective they are at presenting your data. You can create several dashboards, each with its own specific purpose. If you have a dashboard and want to create another similar one, you can save yourself some steps and time by simply cloning an existing dashboard.

To clone a dashboard:

1. Click on the Dashboards tab, or click the more arrow and click Dashboards.
2. Click Go to Dashboard List link on the top-left corner of the Dashboard view and click on the name of the dashboard you want to clone.
3. Click Clone and then follow the steps to customize this dashboard. The steps in Task B in the Dashboards section of this chapter will walk you through the process.
4. You can now select your custom dashboard from the Dashboard List.

Check out the AppExchange, where you can install a number of custom add-on dashboards. Click the AppExchange icon in the upper-right corner of the Salesforce interface.

To clone and edit Dashboards, you'll need **Manage Dashboards** permission.

This feature is available in:

✔ Unlimited	✔ Developer
✔ Enterprise	Group
✔ Professional	Personal

Task D   Editing a dashboard

If you need to view and analyze data changes, you can edit your dashboard views to reflect your new requirements for your data. If you don't want to permanently edit the dashboard, you might consider creating a new dashboard or cloning an existing one. Both topics are covered in earlier tasks in this section.

When editing a dashboard, you can change the size of columns, add or delete components, change the way data is displayed, as well as change the look and feel of the different dashboard components.

To edit Dashboards, you'll need **Manage Dashboards** permission.

To edit a dashboard:

1. Click on the Dashboards tab, or click the more arrow and click Dashboards.
2. Click Go to Dashboard List link on the top-left corner of the Dashboard view and click on the name of the dashboard you want to edit.
3. Click Edit.
4. In the column you want to edit, click the Edit link.
5. Add or change any of the information in the three steps and click Save.
6. Back in the Dashboard Edit view, click Done.

This feature is available in:

✔ Unlimited	✔ Developer
✔ Enterprise	Group
✔ Professional	Personal

Task E   Deleting dashboards

If you have created a dashboard for a particular, short-term purpose, or you have cloned a dashboard and no longer need the original, you can delete the dashboards you no longer use. This will assist in keeping your list of dashboards clean, so you can quickly and easily navigate to the dashboard you need.

To delete a dashboard:

1. Click on the Dashboards tab, or click the more arrow and click Dashboards.
2. Click Go to Dashboard List link on the top-left of the Dashboard view and click on the Del link next to the name of the dashboard you want to delete.
3. Click OK.

Unlike deleting other elements of Salesforce, you cannot undo the deletion of a dashboard; it does not go into the Recycle Bin, but is instead, really, truly deleted.

To delete Dashboards, you'll need **Manage Dashboards** permission.

This feature is available in:

✔ Unlimited   ✔ Developer
✔ Enterprise   Group
✔ Professional   Personal

Task F   Printing a dashboard

Dashboards are primarily designed as visual tools to help you track and manage business critical information in real time. You may want to print a dashboard to share with colleagues, or just to view in that old-fashioned medium of ink and paper.

To see the latest and greatest data in a dashboard, click the Refresh button.

To print Dashboards, you'll need **Run Reports** permission and access to view dashboard folders.

To print a dashboard:

1. Click on the Dashboards tab, or click the more arrow and click Dashboards.
2. Click Go to Dashboard List link on the top-left corner of the Dashboard view and click on the name of the dashboard you want to print.
3. From the File drop-down on your browser, click Print.
4. Select the printer and then click the Properties button.
5. For your printer, find the place where you can change the orientation to landscape and click OK twice.

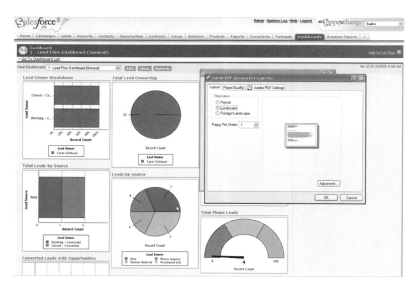

This feature is available in:

✔ Unlimited   ✔ Developer

✔ Enterprise   Group

✔ Professional   Personal

Chapter 12

Working with PDAs

- Access and Setup
- Using Salesforce Mobile on a Windows mobile device
- Using Salesforce on a Blackberry device
- Using Salesforce on your Palm Treo device
- What about my iPhone?

Access and setup

Using Salesforce Mobile, you can see exactly the data you want on your PDA. It is fully customizable. You choose the fields and tabs that are transferred over. Plus, the data is automatically updated—you don't need to do anything. Changes made on your PDA in Salesforce Mobile are instantly uploaded to the web and can be seen on your computer immediately. You do not need to sync to see updates.

Task A Identifying supported PDAs

We all know that new smart phones are introduced to the market all the time. Some of these new phones *may* work with Salesforce. If you want to buy a new phone and want it to use Salesforce Mobile, make sure to check the Salesforce website before your purchase.

To identify which PDAs are supported by Salesforce:

1. Since website URLs can often change, go to www.salesforce.com and type Mobile in the search box.
2. The top result should be Wireless Access to Salesforce. Click on that link.
3. On the right side of the page, you will see a link called Getting Started Salesforce Mobile. Click on that link.
4. This page will provide the most updated list of supported PDAs. At the time of this book printing, the list includes:

   - Select Windows Mobile devices including Treo 700wx and Cingular 8125 and 8525 running version 5 or 6; minimum of 5MB of free memory.
   - Palm OS devices like the popular Treo 600, 650, 680, 700, 750, and 755; minimum of 5MB of free memory.
   - Blackberry devices with OS of 4.0 or higher—the 7000 and 8000 series models; minimum of 2-3 MB of free memory.
   - iPhone will sync using Outlook edition and not Salesforce Mobile.

If you are using a Windows Mobile device, it is strongly recommended that you contact a Salesforce Mobile expert to confirm if your device is supported.

Each PDA will have different memory configurations and capacities. To avoid overloading your PDA, you can specify a maximum data size for each mobile configuration.

To install Salesforce Mobile, you'll need to be able to download an application from the web onto your PDA.

This feature is available in:

✔ Unlimited	Developer
$ Enterprise	Group
$ Professional	Personal

Task B Setting up your PDA

Once you set up your mobile device, all of the data that you want to see will automatically stay updated on your PDA. For example, if you add a contact in Salesforce on your computer, that new contact information will automatically be transferred to your PDA—you don't need to sync, it just happens.

To set up your PDA to view your data:

1. Your Salesforce administrator will send you an email with a link to open a web page. This link will get you to the Salesforce Mobile installer.
2. Select the Click here to download the installer option.
3. This will install the Salesforce Mobile application directly on your PDA.
4. Once this is complete, navigate to your list of applications and open Salesforce Mobile.
5. You will need to accept the licensing agreement.
6. Enter your Salesforce username and password and then select Activate to register your mobile device with Salesforce. Once your login credentials have been verified, your data will start downloading to your PDA. This initial download may take a few minutes so be patient. All future updates occur automatically.
7. After the download, you will be asked to login again.

If you cannot receive the email from your administrator for any reason, you can access the installer link at http://mobile.salesforce.com/setup.

Each PDA will have a different location for the Salesforce Mobile icon. For the Blackberry, look for it in your Application folder or on the home page. For the Windows Mobile device, click Start | Programs | Salesforce Mobile. For the Palm Treo, select InstallAXM icon from the list of applications.

To install Salesforce Mobile, you'll need to be able to download an application from the web onto your PDA.

This feature is available in:

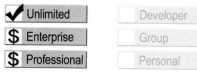

Task C Setting up available data on your PDA

You can determine which tabs of data you want to see on your PDA. So, as a sales person, you may want to see Leads, Accounts, Contacts, and Opportunities but not Cases or Solutions. Not a problem; you can add, remove, or edit any dataset to get these tabs of information.

In general, you should have your Salesforce administrator set up the appropriate dataset for you. If you need to do it yourself, make sure to read the complete Mobile Implementation Guide, which you can access from the Mobile Configuration page.

Just like you can use filters for your list views, you can set up filter criteria so the data that transfers to your PDA is limited by that criteria. For example, you can set a filter so you only see opportunity records with amounts greater than $10,000.

🔒 To view mobile configurations, you'll need **View Setup and Configuration** permission.

🔒 To create, change, or delete mobile configurations, you'll need **Manage Mobile Configurations** permission.

To set up data on your PDA:

1. You will first need to create a mobile configuration. Mobile configurations are the set of parameters that determine what data will be transmitted to your PDA.

2. You should work with your Salesforce administrator to set up a custom configuration, if that is needed. Otherwise, you can use the default configuration that is provided by Salesforce.

3. To define what data you want to see on your PDA, log into your Salesforce account. Click the Setup link at the top of the page.

4. Click the Mobile Administration link on the left side and then click Mobile Configurations.

5. Click on the name of the mobile configuration and then click Edit.

6. From this page, you can add, remove, or edit a dataset.

7. To add a dataset, click Edit and select the data you want to bring over. Once you have selected the data, click OK.

This feature is available in:

✔ Unlimited	Developer	
$ Enterprise	Group	
$ Professional	Personal	

Using Salesforce Mobile on a Windows mobile device

Having all of your contact, opportunity, report, etc., information available to you on your phone is becoming more and more critical for sales people. You can use your Pocket PC to log call information and view your sales opportunities and reports. Best of all, any changes you make are instantly available in Salesforce.com for others to see.

Task A   Making a call

You can use the Salesforce Mobile application to make calls from your Pocket PC and then log the results of those calls. Making a call using Salesforce Mobile certainly has more steps than making a traditional call using your Contacts application so you will probably only use this when you want to see additional details for that contact or log the call results.

To make a call from your Pocket PC:

1. Tap the Start icon to see the list of applications.
2. Tap the Salesforce Mobile option.
3. Enter your password (your username will already be there) and then tap Login.
4. In the search window to the left of the magnifying glass, type in the name of the person you are looking for and then tap the magnifying glass.
5. Your search results will give you all of the information about the name you typed in. Tap on the name under the Contacts section.
6. Tap Actions and then tap Open to get into the contact information.
7. Tap Actions and then place a call on the phone number you want to dial and the call will be initiated. Once the call is completed, you can log the results.

You can use the Search Results drop-down on the right side to find recent searches. This will greatly assist you if you look up the same person or information frequently. You will also see these most recent searches on the Home page when you first log into Salesforce Mobile.

If you want to move contact information to Outlook, under the Actions menu, you can tap Export to Outlook Mobile. If you are syncing your Mobile device with Outlook, that information will be available in your Contacts application as well. This would greatly decrease the number of steps needed to make a call to that person but you cannot log the call when using the Mobile Contacts.

To make a call, you'll need to have Salesforce Mobile installed on your device as well as a Mobile license.

This feature is available in:

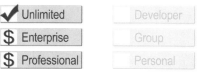

✔ Unlimited	Developer
$ Enterprise	Group
$ Professional	Personal

Task B Logging call information

Once you have completed a call, you can then log that call information into Salesforce Mobile. The information is then instantly available in Salesforce. By doing this, you never have to worry about forgetting what you talked about with someone.

To log a call:

1. Once your call is completed, you will be prompted to log the call, tap Yes.
2. Type in the key information from that call under comments. You can add priority, activity type, etc.
3. Once you have entered the information, tap Save.
4. The information is immediately transferred to your Salesforce database.

Note the type-ahead functionality when you type in the information you want to log. This will really help with getting the notes you want without a lot of typing on your Mobile device.

To log a call, you'll need to have Salesforce Mobile installed on your device as well as a Mobile license.

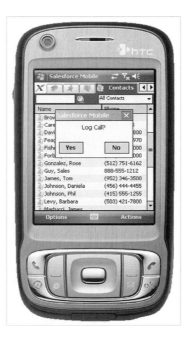

This feature is available in:

✓ Unlimited	Developer
$ Enterprise	Group
$ Professional	Personal

Task C | Viewing and updating sales opportunities

You just closed a major deal and you want to get the results into Salesforce. You can easily do this via your Pocket PC.

To view and update your sales opportunities:

1. Tap the Start icon to see the list of applications.
2. Tap the Salesforce Mobile option.
3. Enter your password (your username will already be there) and then tap Login.
4. Tap on the Opportunity tab. In the search window to the left of the magnifying glass, type in the name of the opportunity you are looking for and then tap the magnifying glass.
5. If your search results yield more than one opportunity by that name, tap on the correct one.
6. Tap the Actions button and then tap Open.
7. You will see the details of this opportunity and can make any needed changes or updates. Tap Actions and tap Edit to make those changes.
8. Once you have completed all of your changes, tap Save. Again, these changes are immediately viewable in Salesforce.

To view your sales opportunities, you'll need to have Salesforce Mobile installed on your device as well as a Mobile license.

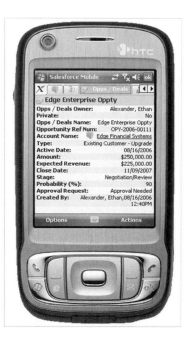

This feature is available in:

✔ Unlimited	Developer
$ Enterprise	Group
$ Professional	Personal

Task D Viewing reports

While you can see any of your reports on your Windows Mobile device, remember that the screen size of your PDA is much smaller than your computer monitor. As a result, it can be difficult to easily view the report information.

To view a report:

1. Tap the Start icon to see the list of applications.
2. Tap the Salesforce Mobile option.
3. Enter your password (your username will already be there) and then tap Login.
4. Tap on the Reports tab header.
5. While you can use the search window to look for a specific report, you can also scroll through the list of reports.
6. Once you see the report you want, tap that report.
7. Tap Action and then tap Open.
8. Tap Action and then tap Refresh data.
9. Once you are finished with the report, tap Save.

You can adjust the size of the column headers for the report by tapping on the bar that separates each column and then dragging that to the left or right. The way you do this is exactly as you would in Excel or other similar spreadsheet applications.

To view reports, you'll need to have Salesforce Mobile installed on your device as well as a Mobile license.

This feature is available in:

✔ Unlimited	Developer
$ Enterprise	Group
$ Professional	Personal

Using Salesforce on a Blackberry device

Having all of your contact, opportunity, report, etc. information available to you on your phone is becoming more and more critical for sales people. You can use your Blackberry to log call information and view your sales opportunities and reports. Best of all, any changes you make are instantly available in Salesforce for others to see.

Task A   Making a call on a Blackberry

You can use the Salesforce Mobile application on your Blackberry to make calls and then log the results of those calls. Making a call using Salesforce Mobile certainly has more steps than making a traditional call using your Contacts application so you will probably only use this when you want to see additional details for that contact or log the call results.

To make a call from your Blackberry:

1. Using your scroll wheel, find Salesforce Mobile and click to open it.
2. Enter your password (your username will already be there) and then click Login.
3. In the search window to the left of the magnifying glass, type in the name of the person you are looking for and then click the magnifying glass.
4. Your search results will give you all of the information about the name you typed in. Scroll to the name you want under the Contacts section and click on it.
5. Scroll to the menu and choose Open to get into the contact information.
6. Scroll to the menu and then choose place a call on the phone number you want to dial, and the call will be initiated. Alternatively, scroll directly to the Place a call from the menu and click on it. Once the call is completed, you can log the results.

You can use the Search Results drop-down to find recent searches. This will greatly assist you if you look up the same person or information frequently. You will also see the most recent searches on the Home page when you first log into Salesforce Mobile.

To make a call, you'll need to have Salesforce Mobile installed on your device as well as a Mobile license.

This feature is available in:

✔ Unlimited	Developer
$ Enterprise	Group
$ Professional	Personal

Task B   Logging a call on a Blackberry

Once you have completed a call, you can then log that call information into Salesforce Mobile. The information is then instantly available in Salesforce. By doing this, you never have to worry about forgetting what you talked about with someone.

To log a call on a Blackberry:

1. Once your call is completed, you will be prompted to log the call. Scroll to Yes and click on it.
2. Type in the key information from that call under the Comments section. You can add priority, activity type, etc.
3. Once you have entered the information, scroll to Save.
4. The information is immediately transferred to your Salesforce database.

The data is saved locally on your Blackberry. Assuming you have wireless coverage, the data is also transmitted directly to Salesforce. If you don't have wireless coverage at the time you make the change, the information is stored on your device and will automatically be transferred once wireless coverage is re-established.

When you log a call, you can also relate that call to a specific contact or opportunity.

To log a call, you'll need to have Salesforce Mobile installed on your device as well as a Mobile license.

This feature is available in:

✔ Unlimited		Developer
$ Enterprise		Group
$ Professional		Personal

Task C   Viewing and updating opportunities on a Blackberry

You just closed a major deal and you want to get the results into Salesforce. You can easily do this via your Blackberry device.

To view and update your sales opportunities:

1. Click the Start icon to see the list of applications.
2. Click the Salesforce Mobile option.
3. Enter your password (your username will already be there) and then click Login.
4. Scroll to the Opportunity tab. In the search window to the left of the magnifying glass, type in the name of the opportunity you are looking for and then scroll to the magnifying glass and click on it. You can also scroll down to the list of all of the opportunities to find the one you want.
5. If your search results yield more than one opportunity by that name, scroll to the correct one and click on it.
6. Scroll to the menu and then click on Open.
7. You will see the details of this opportunity and can make any needed changes or updates. Scroll to the menu and choose Edit to make those changes.
8. Once you have completed all of your changes, scroll to Save and click on it. Again, these changes are immediately viewable in Salesforce.

To view your sales opportunities, you'll need to have Salesforce Mobile installed on your device as well as a Mobile license.

This feature is available in:

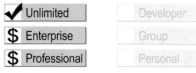

Task D Viewing reports

While you can see any of your reports on your Blackberry device, remember that the screen size of your PDA is much smaller than your computer monitor. As a result, it can be difficult to easily view the report information.

To view a report:

1. Follow the instructions from earlier in the chapter for making a call to log into Salesforce Mobile.
2. Scroll to the Reports tab header.
3. While you can use the search window to look for a specific report, you can also scroll through the list of reports.
4. Once you see the report you want, click on it.
5. Scroll to the menu and click on Open.
6. Once in the report, scroll to the menu and click on Refresh data.
7. Once you are finished with the report, scroll to Save or just scroll to another tab.

If the data exceeds the column size, you can scroll to that field and then the data is visible at the top.

To view reports, you'll need to have Salesforce Mobile installed on your device as well as a Mobile license.

This feature is available in:

✔ Unlimited	Developer
$ Enterprise	Group
$ Professional	Personal

Using Salesforce on your Palm Treo device

Having all of your contact, opportunity, report, etc. information available to you on your phone is becoming more and more critical for sales people. You can use your Palm Treo to log call information and view your sales opportunities and reports. Best of all, any changes you make are instantly available in Salesforce for others to see.

Task A   Making a call from a Palm Treo

You can use the Salesforce Mobile application to make calls from your Treo and then log the results of those calls. Making a call using Salesforce Mobile certainly has more steps than making a traditional call using your Contacts application so you will probably only use this when you want to see additional details for that contact or log the call results.

To make a call from your Palm Treo:

1. Click on the Application icon to see the list of applications.
2. Scroll to find Apex Mobile and tap on this.
3. Enter your password (your username will already be there) and then tap Login.
4. You will see a list of the available tabs on your Treo. Unlike your desktop computer version of Salesforce, the mobile tabs are not displayed horizontally on your Treo; rather, the tabs display as a list that you can scroll through.
5. Scroll to the appropriate category that has the contact name you are searching for—Leads, for example—and then tap Open.
6. You will see the list of leads. Scroll down until you find the contact you are looking for and tap Open. Alternatively, you can start typing the name you are looking for.
7. Click on the Phone icon within the application to place a call or send an email. Once the call is completed, you can log the results.

To quickly get back to the Home page, click the House icon within the Apex Mobile application. If you want to go back one step, click on the arrow pointing left. These icons are within the Apex Mobile application and are not buttons on your Treo.

To make a call, you'll need to have Salesforce Mobile installed on your device as well as a Mobile license.

This feature is available in:

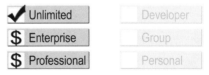

Task B # Logging call information on a Palm Treo

Once you have completed a call, you can then log that call information into Salesforce Mobile. The information is then instantly available in Salesforce. By doing this, you never have to worry about forgetting what you talked about with someone.

To log a call:

1. Once your call is completed, you will be prompted to log the call. Tap Yes.
2. Type in the key information from that call under comments. You can add priority, activity type, etc.
3. Once you have entered the information, tap Save.
4. After saving the information, you are now prompted to schedule a follow-up task. If you tap Yes, you will be taken to the New Event section to add an item to your calendar.
5. The information is immediately transferred to your Salesforce database.

You can easily move between Contacts, Activities, and Opportunities. For example, you can tap on an activity and then go to the contact record of the person related to that activity.

You can also convert leads to Accounts using the menu. Click on the menu and then choose Convert Lead.

To log a call, you'll need to have Salesforce Mobile installed on your device as well as a Mobile license.

This feature is available in:

✔ Unlimited	Developer
$ Enterprise	Group
$ Professional	Personal

Task C   Viewing and updating opportunities on a Palm Treo

You just closed a major deal and you want to get the results into Salesforce. You can easily do this via your Treo.

To view and update your sales opportunities on a Palm Treo:

1. Follow the instructions from earlier in the chapter for making a call to log into Salesforce Mobile.
2. Scroll down to the Opportunities and tap Open.
3. You can either scroll to find the opportunity you are looking for or start typing it.
4. Once you find the opportunity, tap Open.
5. You will see the details of this opportunity and can make any needed changes or updates. Click on the menu and tap Edit to make those changes.
6. Once you have completed all of your changes, tap Save. Again, these changes are immediately viewable in Salesforce.

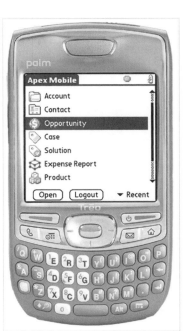

By clicking the menu, you can change ownership for an opportunity. This really brings the functionality of Salesforce to your Treo.

To view your sales opportunities, you'll need to have Salesforce Mobile installed on your device as well as a Mobile license.

This feature is available in:

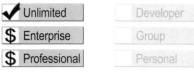

Task D   Adding an activity to your calendar

In Salesforce Mobile, your calendar is called Event. From this section, you can view your calendar and add and change items. It is important to remember that this calendar is separate from the calendar application on your Treo and can only be accessed through the Apex Mobile application.

To add a meeting to your calendar:

1. Click on the Application icon to see the list of applications.
2. Scroll to find Apex Mobile and tap on this.
3. Enter your password (your username will already be there) and then tap Login.
4. Scroll down to Event and tap Open.
5. Tap New; this will open the New Event screen.
6. The default calendar item is assigned to you.
7. Under the subject, you can change it from Meeting to Call or other activity.
8. Scroll or tap to each item and set the day, time, location, and comments for the meeting.
9. Once you are finished, tap Save.

Within the New Event section, you can connect this activity with a specific opportunity by tapping on the Related To link. This means you can see this activity when you go to that opportunity.

To view and change your calendar, you'll need to have Salesforce Mobile installed on your device as well as a Mobile license.

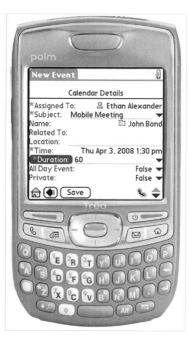

This feature is available in:

✔ Unlimited   Developer

$ Enterprise   Group

$ Professional   Personal

What about my iPhone?

The operating system that works with the iPhone only syncs with Outlook. As a result, you cannot use Salesforce Mobile with an iPhone. You can, however, set up Outlook to sync with Salesforce and then your iPhone will sync with Outlook.

Task A | Setting up an iPhone with Salesforce

You are not really setting up your iPhone to sync with Salesforce. Rather, you are setting up Outlook to sync with Salesforce. This means that the automatic updates occur between Outlook and Salesforce and not your iPhone. Your iPhone only gets updated when you sync it to Outlook.

To set up your iPhone with Salesforce:

1. You will need to first set up the Connect for Microsoft Outlook.
2. Follow the instructions in Chapter 7, "Sending Email."
3. Make sure to set up the synchronization to bring into Outlook all of the items you want to see on your iPhone.
4. Once Outlook has all of your contacts and calendar items, sync your iPhone with Outlook as usual.

If you have never synced your iPhone with Outlook, follow the instructions from Apple on this setup. iPhone setup is very easy and the synchronization begins as soon as you plug your iPhone into the provided sync cable.

This feature is available in:

✔ Unlimited   ✔ Developer
✔ Enterprise   ✔ Group
✔ Professional ✔ Personal

Chapter 13

Working Offline

- Getting Started
- Working with Offline Edition

Getting started

While Internet access is more accessible from more locations everyday, there are still times and places where you need to see the data in Salesforce but don't have a connection to the Internet. Force.com's Offline Edition downloads your key information to your local computer so you can take it with you anywhere.

Task A Installing Offline Edition

In order to use the Offline Edition, you need to install an application to your computer. The installation is quick, easy, and painless.

To install Offline Edition:

1. Log into Salesforce and click Setup | Desktop Integration | Force.com Connect Offline.
2. Click Install Now.
3. Click Yes when prompted to install and run the client.
4. The wizard will walk you through the installation process.
5. Once complete, click Finish.
6. The installation takes less than a minute.

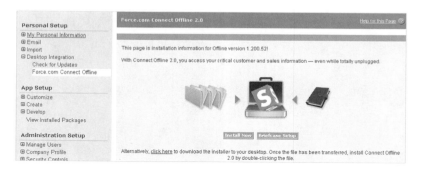

You need to have Internet Explorer 6.0 or 7.0 as well as Windows XP, Vista, or 2000 operating systems. Your computer should have at least 256MB of RAM (recommend at least 512MB), 20MB of free disk space, and a P2 500Mhz processor. Any computer manufactured after 2005 should meet these criteria. In addition, you will need to have permissions to install software on your machine.

🔒 To view records in Offline Edition, you'll need **Read** permission on **Contacts**.

🔒 To update records in Offline Edition, you'll need **Create, Edit, or Delete** permission on **Contacts**.

This feature is available in:

Task B   Logging into Offline Edition

Logging into Offline Edition is a bit different from logging into the online version. You need to have a security key that you insert after your normal password in order to properly authenticate.

To log into Offline Edition:

1. You need to have a security token when you log in. This is Salesforce's way of providing additional security so only valid users are logging into your data.

2. If you do not have/know your security token, log into the online version of Salesforce.

3. Click on Setup | My Personal Information | Reset Security Token.

4. Click the Reset Security Token button. A new security token will be emailed to the email address associated with your Salesforce account.

5. Open your email and copy this new security token information.

6. From the machine where you have installed Offline Edition, click Start | Programs | Salesforce.com | Offline Edition 2.0.

7. Enter your username. For your password, enter your password immediately followed by your security token and click Login. Once you have successfully logged in, the program files will download and the Offline Edition will open. You will need this security token each time you login.

At the login dialog box for Offline Edition, you can click the Update tab names and Synchronize my data check boxes. This will automatically refresh the data in your offline copy of Salesforce.

Since the security token is a very long string of characters, the best way to ensure you are entering it correctly is to copy and paste it into the password field. Depending on your security concerns, you may also want to click the Save Password checkbox; otherwise, you will need to enter the security token each time you log in to Offline Edition.

To view records in Offline Edition, you'll need **Read** permission on **Contacts**.

To update records in Offline Edition, you'll need **Create, Edit or Delete** permission on **Contacts**.

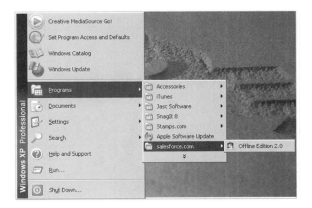

This feature is available in:

✔ Unlimited   ✔ Developer
✔ Enterprise   Group
$ Professional   Personal

Task C   Setting up your briefcase

Your offline briefcase consists of a defined set of accounts, contacts, opportunities, and leads. There are specific criteria that determine what goes into the briefcase. For example, you are limited to a maximum of 4,000 leads and tasks/events from the past two months through the next 24 months.

When you are editing the briefcase settings, note there is a Click here link. This link will provide detailed information as to the information included in the drop-down choices.

To view records in Offline Edition, you'll need **Read** permission on **Contacts**.

To update records in Offline Edition, you'll need **Create, Edit** or **Delete** permission on **Contacts**.

To set up your briefcase:

1. Log into your online version of Salesforce.
2. Click Setup | Desktop Integration | Force.com Connect Offline.
3. Click the Briefcase setup button. Click Edit Briefcase Settings.
4. From the drop-down, choose the information you want to include in your briefcase.
5. Click Save.
6. The next time you log into Offline Edition, that new information will be available.

This feature is available in:

188

Task D Updating the data in Offline Edition

Since the data in your Offline Edition is only as current as the last time you updated it, it is important to update it as frequently as you can. The process is easy and only takes a few minutes.

To refresh or update the data in your Offline Edition:

1. You must be connected to the Internet to update your data.
2. Log into Offline Edition.
3. In the top-right corner, click Synchronize Briefcase.
4. A connection is established with your online version and any changes are brought over to your offline version.

You can avoid this entire step if you have the Synchronize data box checked when you first log into Offline Edition. But remember, you need to be connected to the Internet to send and receive the changes.

🔒 To view records in Offline Edition, you'll need **Read** permission on **Contacts**.

🔒 To update records in Offline Edition, you'll need **Create, Edit or Delete** permission on **Contacts**.

This feature is available in:

Task E | Manually removing accounts

You can manually remove any account that you manually added. You would want to do this when you find you don't need that account information any longer or if you have exceeded the limits of Offline Edition and need to trim out some accounts.

To manually remove accounts from your briefcase:

1. Log in to your online Salesforce account. Click Setup | Desktop Integration | Connect Offline.
2. Click Briefcase Setup.
3. To remove an account, click the checkbox next to that account and then click Remove from Briefcase.
4. The next time you update your briefcase, all of the accounts you have selected for deletion will be removed, including any related contacts, activities, opportunities, or custom object records.

To view records in Offline Edition, you'll need **Read** permission on **Contacts**.

To update records in Offline Edition, you'll need **Create, Edit or Delete** permission on **Contacts**.

This feature is available in:

✔ Unlimited   ✔ Developer
✔ Enterprise   Group
$ Professional   Personal

Task F   Manually adding accounts

While the default briefcase may contain most of the account information you need, you may find you need additional accounts. You can manually add these accounts to your briefcase.

To manually add accounts to your Offline Edition:

1. Log in to your online Salesforce account.
2. Click on the Accounts tab and then search for the account you want to add to Offline Edition.
3. Click on that account to get to the Account Detail view.
4. Click the Include Offline button. The next time you update your briefcase, this account will be included.

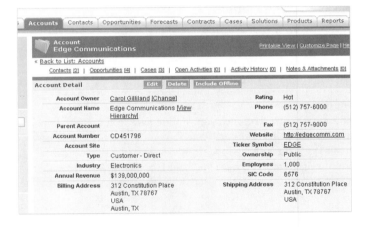

When you add an account to Offline Edition, all of the related contacts, opportunities, and activities are also added. There are limitations to the related information that comes over—you must have read access to the contacts and opportunities and the tasks and events have time limitations.

Your briefcase size has some limitations—the maximum number of leads is 4,000 and accounts is 5,000. In addition, events and tasks have some time limitations—from the past two months through the next 24 months.

To view records in Offline Edition, you'll need **Read** permission on **Contacts**.

To update records in Offline Edition, you'll need **Create, Edit or Delete** permission on **Contacts**.

This feature is available in:

Working with Offline Edition

Working with the Offline Edition is as easy as working with the online edition. In fact, at times, you may forget you are offline. While you don't have access to all of the information in the online edition, the Offline Edition gives you access to key information like phone numbers, addresses, and notes about the various contacts, accounts, and opportunities.

Task A Navigating Offline Edition

Navigating around the Offline Edition is almost identical to using the online version. Remember that it is critical to synchronize your briefcase whenever you can get an Internet connection—that will ensure your data is the most up to date.

To navigate the Offline Edition:

1. To navigate around the Offline Edition, you will click on the various tabs, exactly as you do with the online version.
2. On the Home tab, you can view, create, modify, or delete any of your events.
3. By clicking on the Briefcase Info, you can see the number of contacts, opportunities, etc. assigned to your briefcase.
4. To update your offline data with your online data, you can click the Synchronize button above the errors link or click Synchronize Briefcase in the top-right corner. Both clicks accomplish the same thing.
5. When you navigate to the other tabs that are available, you'll notice the information is almost identical to the online version as well.

Note that automatically generated fields like formula fields or auto-numbering fields are not available with the Offline Edition.

To view records in Offline Edition, you'll need **Read** permission on **Contacts**.

To update records in Offline Edition, you'll need **Create, Edit or Delete** permission on **Contacts**.

This feature is available in:

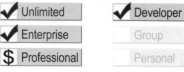

✔ Unlimited   ✔ Developer

✔ Enterprise   Group

$ Professional   Personal

Task B   Emptying your briefcase

By emptying your briefcase, you can get a fresh download of data from your online version of Salesforce. This can be very important when heading out on the road.

To empty your briefcase:

1. Log in to Offline Edition.
2. In the top-right corner, click Empty Briefcase.
3. Click OK to confirm you want to do this.
4. You will need to close out of Offline Edition and log back in.
5. After logging in again, your briefcase is automatically updated with your latest online information.

emobile

| ccounts | Contacts | Opportunities |

Leads
Home

View: All Open Leads   Go!

Recent

Microsoft Internet Explorer

Are you sure you want to empty the contents of your briefcase?

OK   Cancel

Rogers, Jack	Burlington Textiles Corp of America
Owenby, Pamela	Hendrickson Trading
Monaco, David	Blues Entertainment Corp.
Mcclure, Brenda	Cadinal Inc.

The primary reason you want to empty your briefcase is to eliminate any data conflicts when you next synchronize your briefcase. If you have made a lot of changes to your online version of Salesforce, you want to push that updated information to your offline version without conflict. Emptying your briefcase is the fastest, easiest way to get information to your offline version.

To view records in Offline Edition, you'll need **Read** permission on **Contacts**.

To update records in Offline Edition, you'll need **Create, Edit or Delete** permission on **Contacts**.

This feature is available in:

✔ Unlimited   ✔ Developer

✔ Enterprise   Group

$ Professional   Personal

Task C   Resolving data conflicts

During the synchronization process, data from your Offline Edition is compared with that of the online version. Wherever it finds a conflict in the data, the synchronization will stop and you will be asked to choose which data "wins."

One of the primary reasons to empty your briefcase is to avoid the data conflict resolution. One way to minimize this is to synchronize your briefcase as soon as you get back from being out of the office. Then, just prior to heading out again, open the Offline Edition and empty your briefcase. This will give you an updated briefcase to take with you on the road.

To view records in Offline Edition, you'll need **Read** permission on **Contacts**.

To update records in Offline Edition, you'll need **Create, Edit or Delete** permission on **Contacts**.

To resolve conflicts between online and offline data:

1. If the same data has been changed in the offline and online editions of Salesforce, when you synchronize your briefcase, you will see the Salesforce Conflict Resolution dialog box.

2. There are several key columns of information—the field name that has the conflicting information; the Your Values, which is the data from Offline Edition; and the Salesforce Values, which is the data from the online edition.

3. For each item on the conflict list, click the radio button next to the correct information.

4. Once you have clicked on all of the correct information, click Submit.

5. The synchronization of the data will finish and the corrected information will be in both versions—offline and online.

This feature is available in:

✔ Unlimited   ✔ Developer

✔ Enterprise   Group

$ Professional   Personal

Chapter 14

Outlook Integration

- Installing Force.com Connect for Outlook
- Sending emails to Salesforce leads and contacts
- Linking Outlook activities to Salesforce
- Sharing Outlook and Salesforce contacts
- Synchronizing Outlook and Salesforce

Installing Force.com Connect for Outlook

Force.com Connect for Outlook is a separate application that you can install on your desktop PC. It's free for Salesforce users, and it lets you easily send data back and forth between Outlook and Salesforce.

Task A   Backing up your existing Outlook data

If you already have a lot of contact data in Outlook, it's probably a good idea to make sure there is a backup of your Outlook contacts before integrating with Salesforce. These instructions will work for single users of Outlook, so if you are using Outlook with an Exchange server, check with your administrator to make sure your data is backed up. These instructions assume you are using Outlook 2007, but Salesforce works with 2002, 2003, and 2007.

To back up your Outlook data:

1. In Outlook, click File | Data File Management.
2. In the Data Files tab, you'll see a list of your current Outlook data files.
3. Most likely, you'll see a data file called Personal Folders. Highlight your data file and click the Settings button. You should see the location of your PST file.
4. Go to the folder that houses your PST file and make a copy of it in a secure place. The PST file contains all of your Outlook messages, as well as calendar information and contact data.

If you connect to an Exchange server, you may need to ask your network administrator for assistance backing up your existing data. For exchange users, data is stored on the server and not locally in a PST file.

You do not need any special security permissions in Salesforce to complete this task.

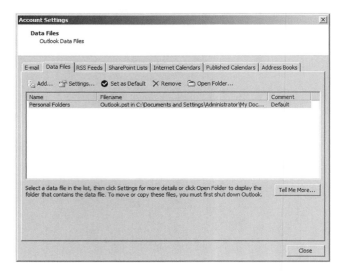

This feature is available in:

✔ Unlimited	Developer
✔ Enterprise	✔ Group
✔ Professional	✔ Personal

Task B   Installing Connect for Outlook

Connect for Outlook is a program that needs to be installed on your local computer to function properly. You will need install rights on your local computer.

To install Connect for Outlook:

1. In the upper-right corner of Salesforce, click the Setup link.
2. On the left, click the Desktop Integration option.
3. Click Connect for Outlook.
4. Click the Install Now button.
5. Follow the instructions to install Connect for Outlook.

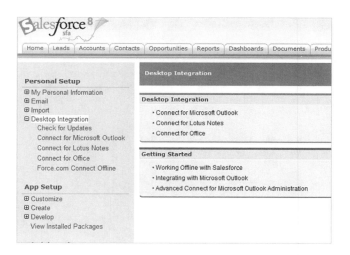

Force.com Connect for Outlook works with:

■ Microsoft Outlook 2002, or newer.
■ Microsoft Windows 2000 or newer.

Connect for Outlook does not work with 64-bit operating systems.

To install software on your local PC, you'll need local install rights. Ask your administrator for assistance if you cannot install programs on your local computer.

Your administrator has the ability to restrict the data that can be transferred into/out of Salesforce with Connect for Outlook.

This feature is available in:

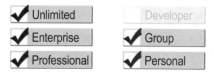

Task C   Configuring Connect for Outlook

The first time you open Outlook after installing Connect for Outlook, a wizard will appear. You can use this wizard to set options for synchronizing your Outlook data with Salesforce. In addition to the settings in this wizard, you can configure settings in Tools | Options within Outlook.

Your administrator has the ability to restrict what you can do with Connect for Outlook. For example, the administrator can restrict your ability to send contacts from Outlook into Salesforce.

Your Salesforce administrator will need to grant you permission to link to Outlook.

To configure Connect for Outlook:

1. You may need to reboot your computer after installing Connect for Outlook. The first time you open Outlook after installing Connect for Outlook, you will be prompted for your username and password.
2. Click Next.
3. You will be prompted to set sync options for contacts, events, and tasks. Your options are: Synchronize with Salesforce, Export to Salesforce, Export with Overwrites to Salesforce, Import from Salesforce, Import with Overrides from Salesforce.
4. Click Next.
5. Select the related entities (opportunities, products, campaigns, cases, etc.) that should be associated with emails sent from Outlook.
6. Click Next.
7. Click Finish.
8. In Outlook, click Tools | Salesforce Options to configure additional options.

This feature is available in:

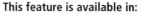

✔ Unlimited   Developer
✔ Enterprise   ✔ Group
✔ Professional   ✔ Personal

Sending emails to Salesforce leads and contacts

Once you have configured Connect for Outlook, emails that are sent from Outlook can be tracked in Salesforce. You can also look up someone's email address (assuming it exists in Salesforce) right from within the Outlook interface. In Outlook, you can send emails to leads, contacts, and person accounts.

Task A   Sending an email to a lead or contact

When Connect for Outlook is installed, a Salesforce Address book is automatically created. You can send emails to anyone in the Salesforce address book, and those emails will be viewable on the contact/lead record back in Salesforce. These instructions assume that you are using Outlook 2007. Check the Salesforce.com help for instructions on sending an email in an older version of Outlook.

To send an email in Outlook to a Salesforce lead or contact:

1. Create a new email message in Outlook.
2. Click the Salesforce.com tab.
3. Click the Salesforce Address Book option.
4. You may be prompted for a username and password. (See the note in the margin about adding the security token to your password.)
5. Type the first and/or last name in the field at the top of the Salesforce Address Book and click the Search option. The contact will appear in the list below.
6. Highlight the contact and click the To button to add the contact to your list of message recipients.
7. Click OK.
8. Type the subject and body of your message.
9. Click the Send and Add button on the Salesforce.com ribbon. If you just click the Send button, your message will not be recorded in Salesforce.

Know your security token! When accessing Salesforce from Connect for Outlook, you must enter your password in the form of <password><security token>. Let's say your password is Green and your security token is 1234. When entering your password for Connect for Outlook, you would enter the password as Green1234. In Salesforce, click Setup | My Personal Information | Reset Security Token if you don't know the security token.

To send an email to a lead, you'll need **Create** permission on **Tasks**.

This feature is available in:

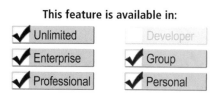

✔ Unlimited	Developer
✔ Enterprise	✔ Group
✔ Professional	✔ Personal

Task B Recording an incoming message in Salesforce

If a contact sends you an important email message, that message lives in your Outlook inbox. You may want to move a record of the email to Salesforce. You can send any email into Salesforce with just a few clicks.

To record an incoming message in Salesforce:

1. Locate the important email message in your Outlook inbox.
2. On the Salesforce toolbar, click the Add Email button.
3. Click the Go! button to find your contact record in Salesforce.
4. When the results of contacts appear, highlight the contact that should be associated with the email message.
5. Click Add to Salesforce.

Emails sent from/received into Outlook show up in Salesforce as a task. To view them, go to the contact or lead in Salesforce and scroll down to the Activity History related list.

To record an incoming message, you'll need **Create** permission on **Tasks**.

Add to Salesforce

Names | Related To | Attachments | Message

Add Email as a New Task
Configure Task Information and Associations

Assigned To: Edd Kachinski   Change | View
Status: Completed
Subject: salesforce

Matching Records (Choose One)

Search: edward@is-crm.com   Go!

Results (double-click to select):

Quick Create: Contact | Lead

Your Name selection: Clear | View

                              Add to Salesforce | Cancel

This feature is available in:

✓ Unlimited   Developer
✓ Enterprise   ✓ Group
✓ Professional ✓ Personal

Linking Outlook activities to Salesforce

If you're working in corporate America, chances are good that you use Microsoft Outlook as your main work calendar. The activities on your Outlook calendar are often scheduled with contacts that are in Salesforce. Because of this, Salesforce has an option to associate Outlook calendar entries and tasks with Salesforce contacts and leads.

Task A   Associating a calendar item in Outlook with a Salesforce contact

When you associate a calendar item in Outlook with a Salesforce contact or lead, you'll see a record of the history when you are viewing the contact in Salesforce.

To associate a calendar item in Outlook with a Salesforce contact:

1. Locate an activity on your calendar in Outlook. Double-click the activity to bring up activity properties.
2. Click the Salesforce.com tab.
3. Click the Associate button on the ribbon.
4. Choose either Contacts or Leads from the Name drop-down.
5. Click Add and select the Salesforce contact that this activity should be associated with.
6. Click OK.

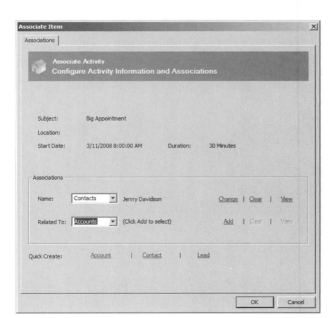

Associated calendar entries do not show up until you perform a synchronization. In Outlook, click the Sync button on the toolbar to synchronize.

To associate a calendar item in Outlook, you'll need **Create** permission on **Tasks**.

This feature is available in:

✔ Unlimited   Developer

✔ Enterprise   ✔ Group

✔ Professional   ✔ Personal

Task B Associating a task in Outlook with a contact in Salesforce

Just like activities on the Outlook calendar can be sent over to Salesforce, tasks can be recorded in Salesforce. The association process is similar for tasks and activities, so if you successfully completed the previous task, this task should follow common sense.

Associated tasks do not show up until you perform a synchronization. In Outlook, click the Sync button on the toolbar to synchronize.

To associate a task, you'll need **Create** permission on **Tasks**.

To associate a task in Outlook with a contact in Salesforce:

1. Create a new task in Outlook.
2. In the task editing screen in Outlook, click the Salesforce.com tab.
3. Click the Associate button on the ribbon.
4. Choose either Contacts or Leads from the Name drop-down.
5. Click Add and select the Salesforce contact that this activity should be associated with.
6. Click OK.

Associate Item				
Associations				

Associate Activity
Configure Activity Information and Associations

Subject: Remember to do the thing
Start Date: 3/17/2008
Due Date: 3/17/2008

Associations

Name: [Contacts ▾] (Click Add to select)   Add | Clear | View

Related To: [Accounts ▾] (Click Add to select)   Add | Clear | View

Quick Create: Account | Contact | Lead

[OK] [Cancel]

This feature is available in:

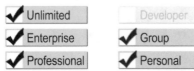

✔ Unlimited	Developer
✔ Enterprise	✔ Group
✔ Professional	✔ Personal

Sharing Outlook and Salesforce contacts

You can send your Salesforce.com contacts into Outlook, and you can mark your Outlook contacts for synchronization back into Salesforce. Then, when you need a phone number, you'll have it in either program.

Task A   Marking an Outlook contact for synchronization to Salesforce

Before you can send a contact from Outlook into Salesforce, you must first associate the Outlook contact with a Salesforce contact or lead.

To configure Outlook/Salesforce integration options:

1. In Outlook, double-click the contact that should be associated with someone in Salesforce.
2. Click the Salesforce.com tab on the ribbon.
3. Click the Associate button on the ribbon.
4. Choose either Contacts or Leads from the Name drop-down.
5. Click Add and select the Salesforce contact that this activity should be associated with.
6. Click Save and Mark for Sync to mark this contact to be synchronized the next time you click the Sync button.
7. Click OK.

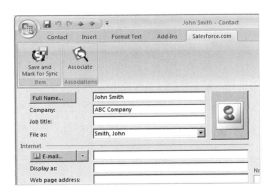

When you synchronize, contacts from Salesforce will automatically show up in Outlook.

In Outlook, click Tools | Synchronize | Contacts tab to set contact synchronization options.

To associate contacts, you'll need **Create** permission on **Contacts**.

This feature is available in:

Synchronizing Outlook and Salesforce

Many of the calendar and contact settings won't be sent between Salesforce and Outlook until you manually synchronize. Luckily, this only requires a single click from within Outlook.

Task A   Performing a synchronization

You will need to be connected to the Internet to synchronize Outlook and Salesforce. A sync can be initiated at any time by clicking the Sync button on the Outlook toolbar.

To initiate synchronization:

1. Make sure Outlook is open. (It should be open to the main Outlook interface, not to a detail page for a contact, email, or task.)
2. Locate the Salesforce toolbar.
3. Click the Sync button.

If you don't see the Salesforce toolbar in Outlook, right-click somewhere on the toolbar and make sure the Salesforce Outlook Edition Main toolbar is checked.

To perform a sync, you'll need **Create** permission on **Contacts** and **Tasks**.

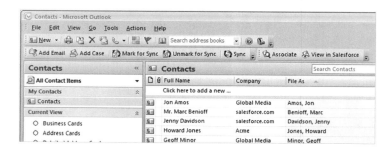

This feature is available in:

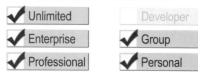

✔ Unlimited	Developer
✔ Enterprise	✔ Group
✔ Professional	✔ Personal

Chapter 15

Extending Salesforce with AppExchange

- Understanding AppExchange
- AppExchange applications for sales people

Understanding AppExchange

The AppExchange is the central location to find add-on products designed to enhance your Salesforce functionality and experience. The applications have been developed by many different companies, including Salesforce.com. These applications can be free, a one-time fee, or an ongoing monthly fee. One of the great things about any application in the AppExchange is you can test drive it for free.

Task A   How to access AppExchange

Since new applications are always being written, it is a great idea to browse the AppExchange on a regular basis to see what's new. You can browse by business solution like IT Management or Marketing, new listings, or the top installs.

To access the AppExchange:

1. Launch Salesforce and log in.
2. In the top-right corner, click the AppExchange logo. This will take you to the AppExchange home page.
3. From here, you can look at the newest applications or the top applications. You can also look at the applications by business need—like dashboards, project management, and more.
4. You can also type in what you are looking for in the search box.
5. Once you find the application you are looking for, click on it for more information and to download a trial.

Since so many of the AppExchange applications are free, you can really extend the value of Salesforce by leveraging them. Set yourself an activity for once a month or once a quarter to browse the AppExchange for ideas.

You actually don't need to log in to your Salesforce account to get to the AppExchange. You can click on it directly from the Salesforce.com home page. You will need to log in if you decide to test drive or buy an application.

This feature is available in:

See Specifications Tab under each AppExchange application to see Editions supported

Task B   Navigating around AppExchange

When you first get to the AppExchange home page, it may seem a bit over-whelming. Instead of closing out the browser, take a deep breath and look at the panel to the left called Find Apps. Find the area that most fits your needs and click on it.

To navigate around AppExchange:

1. Launch Salesforce and then click on the AppExchange.
2. If you are new to the AppExchange, click on the Getting Started tab.
3. Under the Resources tab, you can view presentations on Getting Started with the AppExchange as well as other Online Events.
4. To search for applications, click on the Home tab and either use the search engine or click on one of the other many links.

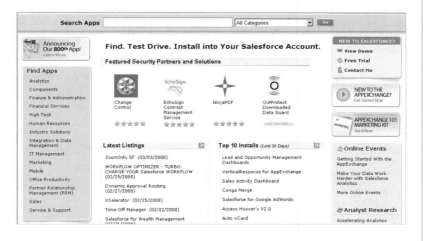

When you click on any application, you will see several tabs, including Overview, Reviews, and Specification. The reviews are great ways to get feedback from other customers on that application. Each review also gives a 5-star rating.

Under the Specifications tab, you will see what version of Salesforce you need in order to use that application. In general, most applications require Professional at a minimum.

This feature is available in:

See Specifications Tab under each AppExchange application to see Editions supported

Before you test drive any application, make sure to view the demo. These demos are typically well done and will give you a great overview of how the application will work.

Task C   Installing AppExchange applications

One of the best things about the applications from the AppExchange is your ability to test drive them before you buy. This gives you a chance to see if the application will really fit your needs.

To install any of the AppExchange applications:

1. Launch Salesforce and then access the AppExchange by clicking on the icon in the top-right corner.
2. Find the application you want to download and click on it.
3. You will see additional information about that application—features, costs, publisher, reviews, additional specs, etc.
4. Click on the Demo or Test Drive to see additional examples or a demo on how the application works.
5. If you think it will meet your needs, you can download it by clicking Get It Now.
6. Depending on the application, you may have to complete a form or log back in to Salesforce. You may have additional installation options.
7. Once you have set up all of the installation options, click the Install button. The application will install into Salesforce and you will be able to use it immediately.

This feature is available in:

See Specifications Tab under each AppExchange application to see Editions supported

AppExchange applications for sales people

Under the Find Apps on the AppExchange home page, you will see Sales. This section lists any application that might be of interest to sales people—from compensation management to sales methodologies to forecasting. It's worth the time to look at the ones that might be of interest to you and your organization.

Task A — Installing an expense report application

For sales people, filling out an expense report can be a major pain and chore. The free Expense Tracker application from Salesforce.com makes it easy. You can set up permissions and authority levels for expense approvals so it is more than just an electronic recap of expenses.

To install an expense report tracker:

1. Launch Salesforce and then click on the AppExchange in the top-right corner.
2. In the search apps window, type expense report and click the Go button.
3. There will be many search results. Click on Expense Tracker. This is a free application from Salesforce.com.
4. Click Test Drive to see how the application works.
5. Click Get It Now to begin the download and installation process.
6. Type in your Salesforce username and password. Select your user type from the drop-down list. Click Continue.
7. Accept the licensing agreement, and click Continue. Then click Next and click Next. Select security settings for who can get this application. Click Next and then click Install. Once you have finished installing the application, it is immediately available for use in Salesforce.

The Expense Tracker is one of the applications that can be downloaded to your PDA. This is awesome for sales people who want to keep track of their expenses while on the road. So, as you incur the expense, you can enter it into your PDA and it is automatically transferred to your Salesforce account.

This feature is available in:

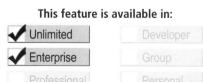

209

Task B Installing additional dashboards

These additional dashboards provide graphical views of your open and closed opportunities. The data is maintained from year to year so you can analyze trends. You can also make these dashboards the view you see when you when you first log in to Salesforce.

If you want to bundle these Lead and Opportunity dashboards with all of the other free dashboards, download the AppExchange Dashboard Pak.

To install additional dashboards:

1. Log in to Salesforce and then click the AppExchange logo in the upper-right corner.
2. In the search window, type dashboards.
3. There will be many search results on this. Click on Lead and Opportunity Management Dashboards. This is a free application from Salesforce.com.
4. Click Test Drive to see dashboard examples.
5. Click Get It Now to begin the installation.
6. Type in your Salesforce username and password. Select your user type from the drop-down list. Click Continue.
7. Accept the licensing agreement. Click Continue, Next, Next, and then Install. Once the installation is complete, the dashboards are immediately available in Salesforce for you to use.

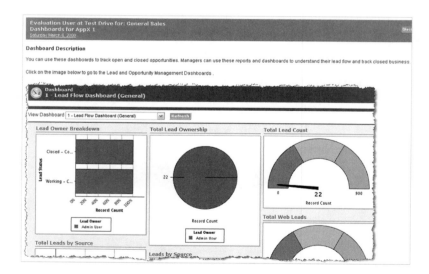

This feature is available in:

Task C   Installing Salesforce for Google AdWords

Using Google AdWords with Salesforce allows you to connect to your existing Google AdWords account or create a new account. You can track all incoming leads and then measure the effectiveness of Google using various lead conversion dashboards.

To install Google AdWords:

1. Launch Salesforce and then click on the AppExchange icon in the top-right corner.
2. In the search window, type Google AdWords.
3. There will be many search results; click Salesforce for Google AdWords.
4. Click Demo to see how this application works.
5. Click the Get It Now option.
6. Type in your Salesforce username and password. Select your user type from the drop-down list. Click Continue.
7. Accept the licensing agreement. Click Continue, Next, Next, Select who can access this information, and then Install. Once the installation is complete, the application is immediately available in Salesforce for you to use.

This application is a tremendous way to track exactly which ads and keywords are generating leads, opportunities, and revenue.

Remember that the Salesforce for Google AdWords is a free application, but you will need to have a valid Google AdWords account and that marketing effort is a for-fee service. In other words, you'll be paying Google for the lead but not paying for the ability to track it within Salesforce.

This feature is available in:

✔ Unlimited   ✔ Developer
✔ Enterprise   ✔ Group
✔ Professional   Personal

Task D Accessing these applications

Now that you have downloaded applications to your Salesforce account, here's how you can view and use them.

To access any of these applications within Salesforce:

1. Log in to Salesforce.
2. You will see that your home page is a bit different now. The new dashboards are the tabs at the top of the Salesforce interface.
3. You can access them in the usual fashion by clicking on the tab.
4. To see all of your tab items, you can click on the arrow that is at the far right of the tabs. This will enable you to see things like Leads, Accounts, Opportunities, etc.
5. When you click on one of the new AppExchange tabs for the first time, depending on the application, you may be prompted to set it up or just start using it.

When you install applications from the AppExchange, your default tabs in Salesforce are replaced by these new applications. To customize your tab view, you can click on the Setup link located at the top right of the screen and then click Customize your tabs and related lists. You can also customize your tabs by clicking the arrow to the right of the tabs and then click the red Customize My Tabs button.

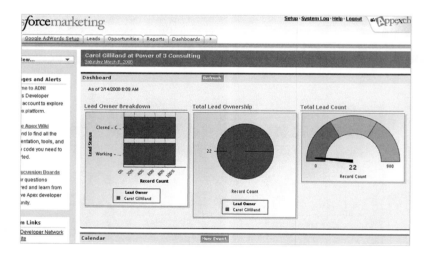

This feature is available in:

See Specifications Tab under each AppExchange application to see Editions supported

Chapter 16

Setting Up Your Database

- Personal setup
- Administrator setup
- Managing your database
- Customizing your database

Personal setup

Customizing and setting up your Salesforce.com database will help increase your efficient use of this valuable tool. By customizing the tabs you see across the top or the quick links on the left side of the screen, you can make Salesforce.com work like you like to work.

Task A   Editing your personal information

When you first set up your Salesforce.com account, the information you provide is stored in your personal information section. You can add to or change this information by editing this section.

Above the User Detail information, you will see some links like Personal Groups, Public Group Membership, etc. By clicking on these links, you jump directly to the edit section for that particular item.

To edit your personal information:

1. Click on the Setup link at the top of your Salesforce.com page.
2. Click on the My Personal Information link on the top-left side under Personal Setup, then click Personal Information. Alternatively, you can click directly on the Edit your information link under the My Personal Information section.
3. Click the Edit button to make changes to your personal profile.
4. Make the appropriate changes to the information.
5. Click Save when finished.

This feature is available in:

✔ Unlimited	✔ Developer
✔ Enterprise	✔ Group
✔ Professional	✔ Personal

Task B | Changing your password

Salesforce.com is only as secure as the password you provide. Make sure to provide a very strong, complex password to help keep others out of your data. By using a combination of uppercase, lowercase, numbers, and special characters, you can help protect yourself.

To change your login password:

1. Click on the Setup link at the top of your Salesforce.com page.
2. Click on the My Personal Information link on the top-left side under Personal Setup, then click on Change My Password. Alternatively, you can click directly on the Change your password link under the My Personal Information section.
3. Type your old password and your new password twice.
4. You will need to verify your security question.
5. Click Save.

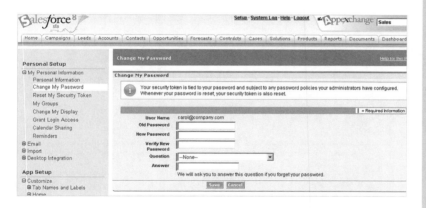

Security is very important for Salesforce.com. You will see this in many areas—whether it is managing access by using security tokens, security questions, or limiting IP addresses that you use to access Salesforce.com. While this certainly helps ensure your data is protected, it can present difficulties in accessing the data if you don't have the proper credentials. Make sure to keep all of your passwords, tokens, and questions/answers in a safe and secure place.

When your password is changed, it also changes your security token. Make sure that you keep track of your new security token as well as your new password.

This feature is available in:

Task C	**Resetting your security token**

A security token is needed to access Salesforce.com when you are not on a trusted network. It is also needed for things like Connect for Outlook, the Offline Edition, Connect for Office, Connect for Lotus Notes, or the Data Loader.

To reset your security token:

1. Click on the Setup link at the top of your Salesforce.com page.
2. Click on the My Personal Information link on the top-left side under Personal Setup, then click Reset My Security Token. Alternatively, you can click directly on the Reset your security token link under the My Personal Information section.
3. An email with your new security token will be sent to the email that is part of your personal information.
4. You will use this new security token when logging into the Offline Edition or when you are outside one of your trusted network sites.

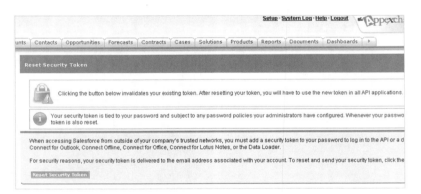

It is very important that you have email access when you make changes to your security token, as you will need to retrieve your new security token before you can log into the Offline Edition or outside a trusted site. It is also a good idea to obtain your security token when you are part of a trusted network.

As a reminder, when logging in using the security token, you will type your password followed immediately by the security token. The security token is a very long string of characters so it is best to keep that information in a secure file so you can just copy/paste it.

This feature is available in:

✔ Unlimited   ✔ Developer
✔ Enterprise   ✔ Group
✔ Professional ✔ Personal

Task D Allowing access for remote technical support

If you ever need remote support from Salesforce.com or from your own IT administrator, you will need to grant them access to your account. This allows them to work on your system until the date you specify.

To allow access for remote technical support:

1. Click on the Setup link at the top of your Salesforce.com page.
2. Click on the My Personal Information link on the top-left side under Personal Setup; then click Grant Login Access. Alternatively, you can click directly on the Grant login access to your administrator or Salesforce.com Customer Support link under the My Personal Information section.
3. Click in the empty date box and a calendar will pop up.
4. Click on the date you want to allow access. This means a Salesforce.com support representative or your database administrator will be able to log into your database until that date.
5. Click Save.

Once you click the Save button, you will see that your Setup page is different and that there is a link to contact customer support. If you click that link, a .pdf on the various ways to get resolution to your support issue will open.

If you find you do not need or want the support any longer, follow the steps under Task D and delete the date; then click Save.

Setup · System Log · Help · Logout

| ounts | Contacts | Opportunities | Forecasts | Contracts | Cases | Solutions | Products | Reports | Documents | Dashboards |

Grant Login Access

Grant login access to salesforce.com Customer Support

To assist you with support issues, a salesforce.com support representative may need to access your data using your login. The support representative will have login access until the expiration date you set below.

User Name carol@po3inc.com
Access Expiration Date `3/21/2008` [3/19/2008]

Grant login access to your administrator

To assist you with support issues, your administrator may need to access your data using your login. Your administrator will have login access until the expiration date you set below.

User Name carol@po3inc.com
Access Expiration Date [3/19/2008]

Save Cancel

This feature is available in:

✔ Unlimited   ✔ Developer
✔ Enterprise   ✔ Group
✔ Professional ✔ Personal

Task E   Sharing your calendar

Your database administrator has probably already set up an organization-wide calendar sharing. The choices you have here are to make your calendar less restrictive only. By changing the access, you can give others more visibility into your activities but not the ability to see the event detail pages.

To see detailed definitions of the meaning of the Calendar Access types, click the Help for the Page link near the top-right side of this page. This will help you make the best choice for which type of calendar share you want to set up for each user and/or group.

To share your calendar with other users:

1. Click on the Setup link at the top of your Salesforce.com page.
2. Click on the My Personal Information link on the top-left side under Personal Setup; then click Calendar Sharing. Alternatively, you can click directly on the Manage the visibility of your calendar to other users link under the My Personal Information section.
3. This will show you the list of users and/or groups that have access to your calendar.
4. To change/add/delete a user or group, click the Add button.
5. From the drop-down, choose the appropriate group or user list. This will populate on the left side of the two boxes below with a list of groups or users.
6. Click on the user or group that you want to have access to your calendar. Click the arrow pointing right to move them to the New Sharing box.
7. Choose the Calendar Access type drop-down and choose the appropriate share level. Click Save.

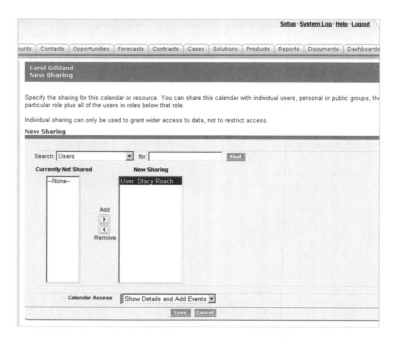

This feature is available in:

✔ Unlimited   ✔ Developer

✔ Enterprise   Group

✔ Professional   Personal

Task F   Updating the My Stay-in-Touch settings

The Stay-in-Touch feature allows for automatic emails to be generated and sent when you add a new contact to your database. This is a quick-and-easy way to request and confirm that you have the correct and most up-to-date phone, email, and address information. You can also send a Stay-in-Touch email directly from the detail page of that contact.

To update the My Stay-in-Touch setting:

1. Click on the Setup link at the top of your Salesforce.com page.
2. Click on the Email link on the top-left side under Personal Setup; then click the My Stay-in-Touch Settings link. Alternatively, you can click directly on the Change our outgoing Stay-in-Touch email settings under the Email section.
3. You can choose to get a BCC on all of your outbound emails, set reminders to email the Stay-in-Touch email to new contacts added to your database, and edit the email you would send out.
4. Make the appropriate selections to customize your Stay-in-Touch.
5. If you want to add additional merge fields directly from your database, near the top, in the blue Available Merge Fields section, select the field you want, then copy it from the Copy Merge Field Value to the appropriate spot in your Stay-in-Touch note.
6. Add any personalized signature. Click Save.

If there is specific data, like a mobile phone number, that you want to make sure is correct for your contacts, you can add that field in your Stay-in-Touch note. This will help to highlight it for that contact when he receives your email so he can verify the accuracy of that information.

To request updates, you'll need **Send Stay-in-Touch Requests** permission.

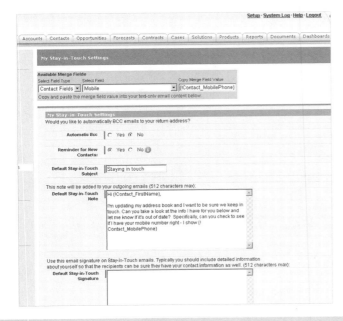

This feature is available in:

Unlimited | Developer
Enterprise | Group
Professional | Personal

Administrator setup

While the information in this section covers some of the key setup items, it is still a good idea to review the Rollout Guide that Salesforce provides. The guide provides best-practice examples and will help ensure a successful implementation of Salesforce.com.

Task A   Setting up your company information

When your company first signs up for Salesforce.com, the information provided for the company is displayed in the Company Information page. In this section, you will also see the total number of licenses for Salesforce.com as well as the additional Salesforce features like Offline Edition.

To set up your company profile:

1. Click on the Setup link at the top of your Salesforce.com page.
2. Click on the Company Profile link on the left side under Administrative setup; then click the Company Information link.
3. Click the Edit button located in the middle of the page.
4. Make the appropriate changes/additions/deletions from this page.
5. Click Save.

This is the section where you choose to receive newsletters from Salesforce as well as notifications about system maintenance and downtime. If you are a Salesforce.com power user, you should make sure the Hide Notices about System Downtime option is deselected.

To view company information, you'll need **View Setup and Configuration** permission.

To change company information, you'll need **Customize Application** permission.

This feature is available in:

✔ Unlimited	✔ Developer
✔ Enterprise	✔ Group
✔ Professional	✔ Personal

Task B   Creating users

Since you are paying every month for every user, you want to make sure to maximize this investment. In this section, you can add users or make current users inactive, which will free up a license for another user.

To create a new user:

1. Click on the Setup link at the top of your Salesforce.com page.
2. Click on the Manage Users link on the left side under Administrative setup; then click the Users link.
3. Click the New User button.
4. Enter the information for the user. As a reminder, the email address is the username. All of the fields with a red bar to the left are required fields.
5. Once you have completed filling out the information, click Save.

The Help for this Page link at the top right of this section is a great resource for understanding how the Roles and Profiles in Salesforce.com work.

If you want to make a user inactive, you need to edit the user and then deselect the Active checkbox on the right side under the Profile drop-down. This will free up a license for another user.

To create, edit, or deactivate users, you'll need **Manage Users** permission.

This feature is available in:

✔ Unlimited   ✔ Developer
✔ Enterprise   ✔ Group
✔ Professional   Personal

Setting up the sharing for users is important to do as soon as you first create your database. This will ensure the users have consistent access to the data from the first time they start using Salesforce.com. In addition, it may take a lot of time and resources to process the changes, depending on the amount of data you have.

Role hierarchies are used to grant additional access beyond what is specifically called out in the access level you choose.

To set default sharing access, you'll need **Manage Users** and **Customize Application** permission.

Task C   Sharing data between users

In this task, you can set up organization-wide sharing for each object. You can also establish if you want to ignore hierarchies when determining the access level. Remember that sharing rules do not apply to private contacts so you don't have to worry about those contacts being viewed by others.

To share data between users:

1. Click on the Setup link at the top of your Salesforce.com page.
2. Click on the Security Controls link on the left side under Administrative setup; then click the Sharing Settings link.
3. Click the Edit button to change the access level by object.
4. Using the drop-downs, make the appropriate changes to the access for each object.
5. Click Save.

This feature is available in:

✔ Unlimited	✔ Developer
✔ Enterprise	Group
✔ Professional	Personal

Task D Setting up access from different computers

Setting up additional trusted IP addresses means you can access Salesforce.com from those locations without needing to use the security token. When you first set up your Salesforce.com account, the IP address that you use is automatically added as a trusted site. Setting up additional trusted sites is for when you are working from different locations.

To set up access from different computers:

1. Click on the Setup link at the top of your Salesforce.com page.
2. Click on the Security Controls link on the left side under Administrative setup; then click the Network Access link.
3. Click the New button.
4. Enter the Start IP address and the End IP address. If that network only has one Static IP address, the start and end IP addresses are the same.
5. Click Save.

Setting up these IP addresses can only be done on networks with static IP addresses. While you can add a dynamic IP address, please remember that those IP addresses are subject to change so it may not always work.

To view network access, you'll need **View Setup and Configuration** permission.

To change network access, you'll need **Manage Users** permission.

This feature is available in:

✔ Unlimited   ✔ Developer
✔ Enterprise   ✔ Group
✔ Professional ✔ Personal

Again, the Help for this Page link at the top right of the page is a super resource for understanding the definitions of each of the policy rules.

If a user becomes locked out, the administrator can view the user's information and unlock, or the user can wait until the lockout period expires.

To set password policies, you'll need **Customize Application** permission.

Task E Setting up a password policy

By setting up a password policy, each user is forced to comply with the resulting security restrictions. You can set a minimum number of characters as well as the complexity that is needed for each password.

To set up a password policy:

1. Click on the Setup link at the top of your Salesforce.com page.
2. Click on the Security Controls link on the left side under Administrative setup; then click the Password Policies link.
3. Click on each of the drop-downs to make the appropriate choices for your organization.
4. Once completed, click the Save button.

This feature is available in:

✔ Unlimited ✔ Developer

✔ Enterprise Group

✔ Professional Personal

Managing your database

Having current, complete, and relevant data in your database will help ensure maximum usage and productivity. Salesforce.com makes that easy with import wizards and tools to mass edit, delete, or move data.

Task A   Importing data into Salesforce.com

Importing data from Outlook, another contact management software, or even an Excel spreadsheet will really help kick-start your database. Salesforce.com has created specific import wizards for Outlook and ACT! (versions 3-6). But any program where the data can be saved as a .csv file (comma separated values) can be imported into Salesforce.com.

To import data:

1. Click on the Setup link at the top of your Salesforce.com page.
2. Click on the Data Management link on the left side under Administrative setup; then click the Import Accounts/Contacts link.
3. It is strongly recommended that you click on each of the Tell me more links for the five- step import process. Once you have done that and are ready to import, click the Start the Import Wizard link.
4. Browse for the .csv file and choose how you want the import to search for duplicate contacts and/or accounts. Click Next.
5. For the next four steps, it is critical that you carefully and correctly map the contact and/or account information from your .csv file to the appropriate Salesforce field.
6. Step 7 allows you to include any field that wasn't mapped in a Contact or Account note.
7. Step 8 is when you start the import. Click the Import Now button. Once the import is complete, you will receive notification via email.

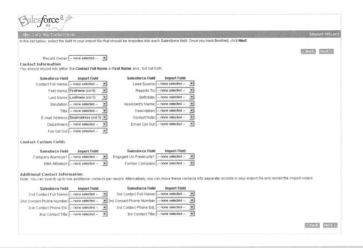

Before you import your entire database into Salesforce.com, do a test import of just a few records. That way, you can verify you have the mapping correct and all of the information properly mapped over.

When importing data from ACT! version 4-6 or Outlook, the Import My Contacts wizard will automatically map those fields from ACT! or Outlook to Salesforce.com.

To import your own person accounts, you'll need **Create** permission on **Accounts**, **Read** permission on **Contacts**, **Import personal contacts** permission, and at least one person account record type available for your profile.

This feature is available in:

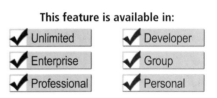

✔ Unlimited   ✔ Developer
✔ Enterprise   ✔ Group
✔ Professional   ✔ Personal

Task B   Transferring data between users

Sales people leave the company and territories realign—sound familiar? Salesforce.com makes it easy to move data between users. You can set the filters on what data you want to move and who you want to move it from and to. When transferring accounts, all of the associated attachments, notes, open activities, etc., are also transferred.

To mass transfer data between users:

1. Click on the Setup link at the top of your Salesforce.com page.
2. Click on the Data Management link on the left side under Administrative setup; then click the Mass Transfer Records link.
3. Click on the type of information you want to transfer. For this example, click on Transfer Leads.
4. Click on the magnifying glass to choose the users to transfer from and to.
5. Set up the filtering criteria for each type of lead to transfer.
6. Click the Find button to see all of the leads that meet your criteria.
7. If you want to transfer all of them, click the Name check box. If you want to individually select the leads to transfer, click the appropriate boxes next to those contact names. Once all of the leads have been selected, click the Transfer button.

Before transferring any records, make sure the new owner has sharing access and at least Read permissions for the record you are transferring as well as the associated records.

Using the Mass Transfer is an easy way to transition leads and accounts when territories shift.

To transfer multiple accounts or leads, you'll need **Transfer Record** permission.

To transfer multiple leads only, you'll need **Transfer Leads** permission.

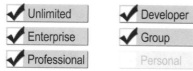

This feature is available in:

✔ Unlimited   ✔ Developer
✔ Enterprise   ✔ Group
✔ Professional   Personal

Task C Mass data deletion

You may need to delete a large number of records due to an incorrect import or duplicate records. Using the Mass Delete function allows you to do this very quickly. When you delete a record, any associated records that display on that record's related lists are also deleted, so make sure to check that information prior to the deletion.

To delete mass data:

1. Click on the Setup link at the top of your Salesforce.com page.
2. Click on the Data Management link on the left side under Administrative setup; then click the Mass Delete Records link.
3. Choose the type of records you want to delete. For this example, click on Mass Delete Contacts. Click Search to proceed.
4. Set up the filtering criteria for the contacts you want to delete.
5. If you want to delete all of them, click the Name check box. If you want to individually select the contacts to delete, click the appropriate boxes next to those contact names.
6. Click the Permanently delete the selected records check box if you don't want the deleted records to go to the Recycle Bin.
7. Once all of the contacts have been selected, click the Delete button.

Before using the mass delete, make a backup of your database. This will create an archive of the information, just in case it is needed in the future.

By setting your filter criteria to Last Modified Date and then choosing less or equal, you can mass delete contacts that you haven't touched in a while. This is a great way to keep only current contacts in your database.

To delete mass data, you'll need **Modify All Data** permission.

Step 1: Review what will happen when you mass delete your Contacts:
This screen allows you to delete a list of Contacts from Salesforce. The following data will also be deleted:

- Contact Notes
- All Opportunities associated with the Contacts
- All Activities associated with the Contacts

Once data is deleted, it will be moved to the Recycle Bin.

Step 2: Recommendation prior to mass deleting:

We strongly recommend you run a report to archive your data before you continue.

It is also strongly advised to request and receive a weekly export of your data before running mass delete. The weekly export service is included with Enterprise Edition, and available for an additional cost with Professional Edition. Contact salesforce.com for more information.

Step 3: Find Contacts that match the following criteria:

Last Modified Date	less or equal	01/01/2005	AND
--None--	--None--		AND
--None--	--None--		AND
--None--	--None--		AND
--None--	--None--		

Filter By Additional Fields (Optional)

- You can use "or" filters by entering multiple items in the third column, separated by commas.
- For date fields, enter the value in following format: 3/19/2008
- For date/time fields, enter the value in following format: 3/19/2008 7:14 AM

Search

Contacts with associated cases will not be deleted.
Contacts with associated active Self-Service users will not be deleted.
Permanently delete

☑ Permanently delete the selected records. When this option is selected, you cannot restore deleted records from the Recycle Bin. Please be careful when selecting this option.

Delete

	Name	Account Name	Title	Phone	Email	Contact Owner Alias	Created By Alias	Last Modified By Alias
☐	Amos, Teri	Universal Media	Sales Manager	(555) 555-1212	info@salesforce.com	MRoac	MRoac	MRoac
☐	Baden, John	Universal Defense Corporation	Senior IT Manager	(555) 555-1212	info@salesforce.com	MRoac	MRoac	MRoac
☐	Banco, Jane	McCall-Janeson Worldwide	Manager	(555) 555-1212		MRoac	MRoac	MRoac

This feature is available in:

✔ Unlimited	✔ Developer
✔ Enterprise	✔ Group
✔ Professional	✔ Personal

Task D Mass address update

Using the Mass Address Update allows you to standardize on the naming convention of countries and states. For example, if you have some users that enter New Jersey and others enter NJ, you can do a mass update to standardize on just one of these. This is very helpful when doing queries because you don't have to query all of the possible names, just the new standard name.

Using this mass address update is a great way to ensure consistent naming of states and countries. This is critical when you are using the filtering criteria based on those two fields because you want to make sure to capture all of the records that are part of that state and/or country.

To mass update addresses, you'll need **Modify All Data** permission.

To mass update addresses of contracts, you'll need **Modify All Data** permission and you'll need **Activate Contracts** permission.

To mass update address information:

1. Click on the Setup link at the top of your Salesforce.com page.
2. Click on the Data Management link on the left side under Administrative setup; then click the Mass Update Addresses link.
3. Let's update the country information for the US. Country is the default selection so click Next.
4. In the Available Values box is a list of all of the different country names in your database. Find each of the names that refer to the United States and click the right arrow add button.
5. Once you have all of the possible country names, type in the name you want for this country in the Replace selected values with box.
6. Click Next. You will see a list of records that will be changed.
7. If the change is acceptable, click Replace. You will get a confirmation that the records were successfully updated.

This feature is available in:

✔ Unlimited   ✔ Developer
✔ Enterprise   ✔ Group
✔ Professional   ✔ Personal

Task E Backing up your database

Some industries are required to keep a backup of their database for compliance purposes. You may also want to keep a backup for your own peace of mind. The backup creates a .csv file of all or parts of the database.

To back up your database:

1. Click on the Setup link at the top of your Salesforce.com page.
2. Click on the Data Management link on the left side under Administrative setup; then click the Data Export link.
3. Click the Click here to download this file link.
4. You can either save or open this file.
5. If you save it, you will be prompted for the folder location. Navigate to the appropriate backup folder and click Save.

You can contact Salesforce directly if you want to receive weekly backups of your database. If you don't choose this service, you may want to schedule an activity for yourself once a week to back up your data.

To back up your data, you'll need **Weekly Data Export** permission.

This feature is available in:

✔ Unlimited	Developer
✔ Enterprise	Group
Professional	Personal

Customizing your database

In Salesforce.com, you can add custom fields as well as set who can see and/or edit any fields in the database. You can customize each of the standard tabs including adding custom fields and setting page layouts.

Task A Adding custom fields

You can add custom fields to the database as well as customize the pick list for any field in the database. You can set the field type to be a phone number, email address, text, etc. Salesforce.com automatically places those new fields on your layout.

To add a custom field:

1. Click on the Setup link at the top of your Salesforce.com page.
2. Click on the Customize link on the left side under App setup; then click the type of information you want to customize. For this example, let's click on Leads.
3. Click on the Fields link on the left side or the Add a custom field to leads under the Lead section.
4. You will see the full list of standard fields at the top. Scroll down to see the list of custom fields. Click the New button to add a custom field.
5. For this example, let's click Text. Then click Next.
6. Provide the field label, length, any description, etc. If you want to set a default value for new leads, enter that under the Default value. Click Next.
7. Click Next. Review the information of the new field and if it is okay, click Save. If you want to add more fields, click Save & New.

One of the settings you can choose is to make a field mandatory. Use this with great care as users will get frustrated if they feel they can't get out of a record without doing a lot of typing. This can result in inaccurate data or users just not wanting to use Salesforce.com.

Salesforce.com does not give you the option to determine where on the record your custom information will go. By creating the field, it is automatically placed on that layout for viewing and editing.

🔒 To create or change custom fields, you'll need **Customize Application** permission.

🔒 To change standard fields, you'll need **Customize Application** permission.

This feature is available in:

✔ Unlimited	✔ Developer
✔ Enterprise	✔ Group
✔ Professional	✔ Personal

Task B Setting field-level security

You can protect important or sensitive data by making those fields read-only or hidden. You will be setting this up based on the specific user profile. This can be very useful if you store information like social security numbers, credit card information, or IP addresses and you only want certain people in the organization to see that information.

To set field-level security:

1. Click on the Setup link at the top of your Salesforce.com page.
2. Click on the Customize link on the left side under App setup; then click the type of information you want to customize. For this example, let's click on Leads.
3. Click on the Fields link on the left side or the Add a custom field to leads under the Lead section.
4. You will see the full list of standard fields at the top. For this example, let's make the phone number read-only.
5. To do this, click on the Phone link. Then click Set Field-Level Security.
6. Click the Read-Only check box. Even though the user permissions will override this setting, it is still a good idea to deselect the System Administrator. You can also deselect any other user like the Support Profile.
7. Click Save.

Even if you limit access to a field, if a user has Modify All Data, View All Data, or View Encrypted Data permissions, those permissions will override the field-level security.

Setting up field-level security is a great way to protect key information from inadvertently being changed. You may want to set up addresses, emails, and phone numbers to be read-only except for the administrative support users.

To set field-level security, you'll need **Customize Application** permission.

Field-Level Security for Profile	Visible	Read-Only
Contract Manager	✓	✓
Custom: Marketing Profile	✓	✓
Custom: Sales Profile	✓	✓
Custom: Support Profile	✓	✓
Marketing User	✓	✓
Read Only	✓	✓
Solution Manager	✓	✓
Standard User	✓	✓
System Administrator	✓	

This feature is available in:

✓ Unlimited   ✓ Developer

✓ Enterprise   Group

Professional   Personal

You can customize each of the different Custom App views. Then, to access these views when working in Salesforce.com, click the drop-down in the top-right corner and choose that view.

If you want to change the name of a tab, for example, let's say you like to use the word "company" instead of "accounts," this also can be done. Go to Setup | Customize | Tab Names and Labels | Rename Tabs and Labels.

To view setup options, you'll need **View Setup and Configuration** permission.

To customize for your organization, you'll need **Customize Application** permission.

Task C   Customizing the tabs

You can customize multiple views of your tabs so you can maximize your efficiency when navigating in Salesforce.com. So, if you don't need to see certain tabs like Cases or Solutions, you can remove them from your view. Conversely, if you add a new tab like Expense Report, you may want to see that on your standard Sales view.

To customize the tabs:

1. To customize which tabs you see at the top and their order from left to right, click on the right pointing arrow at the far right of current tabs. This will take you to the All Tabs view.
2. Click on the red Customize My Tabs button.
3. Choose the Custom App view you want to change. For this example, let's choose Sales.
4. In the left box below the Custom App, add any of the available tabs to the right side.
5. From the right side, by clicking on a tab, you can move it up or down, which will move it to the left or right, respectively, in your tab view.
6. Click Save.

This feature is available in:

✔ Unlimited   ✔ Developer

✔ Enterprise   ✔ Group

✔ Professional   ✔ Personal

Task D   Customizing the home page

When you first log into Salesforce.com, you see your home page. Having your calendar, task list, or dashboards on this page will help remind you of what needs to be done and help keep you on track. This page can be customized so you see only the items that are most relevant to the way you work.

To customize the home page layout:

1. Click on the Setup link at the top of your Salesforce.com page.
2. Click on the Customize link on the left side under App setup; then click Home.
3. Click on Home Page Layouts. To edit your current home page, click the Edit link.
4. Click on the items you want to see on your home page. In Step 1, these are the categories of information and not the specific details. Click Next.
5. In Step 2, you can set the order of how these items will appear on your page. So, if you want your Calendar to be at the top of the page, click on it, then click the Top button.
6. Click Save.

You can add your logo to your home page by clicking on the Home Page Components under the Customize/Home section of the App Setup.

If you add the dashboard to your home page, the dashboard you will see is the last dashboard you accessed.

To view home page, you'll need **Customize Application** permission.

To create or change home page layouts, you'll need **Customize Application** permission.

This feature is available in:

✔ Unlimited   ✔ Developer

✔ Enterprise   ✔ Group

✔ Professional ✔ Personal

Task E   Customize activity settings

Some of the custom activity settings are setting activity reminders, enabling spell checker, email tracking, and the ability to create recurring events. You can also enable a sidebar calendar shortcut on the left side of your screen.

To customize your settings for activities:

1. Click on the Setup link at the top of your Salesforce.com page.
2. Click on the Customize link on the left side under App setup; then click the Activities link.
3. Click on the Activity Settings link.
4. Click on the items you want to see or use with your activities. You can enable spell checker on tasks and events, for example.
5. Click Submit.

The Enable Sidebar Calendar Shortcut will display a shortcut link to your last used calendar view in the sidebar.

Clicking on the Show Events Details on Multi-User Calendar view allows you to see the actual event details on-screen rather than in the mouse-over text view.

Calendar sharing permissions will override the checking of this box. In other words, if you couldn't see another person's calendar, clicking this box will not give you that permission.

🔒 To view activity settings, you'll need **View Setup and Configuration** permission.

🔒 To customize activity settings, you'll need **Customize Application** permission.

This feature is available in:

✔ Unlimited   ✔ Developer
✔ Enterprise   ✔ Group
✔ Professional   ✔ Personal

Index

A

access levels for contacts, 13
account lists
    new account list, creating, 7
    viewing, 6
account teams
    adding users to, 15
    editing team members, 16
accounts. *See also* **account lists;**
    account teams; Google
    AdWords
    access list for account, viewing,
        13
    deleting, 5
    editing, 4
        team members, 16
    hierarchy of accounts, viewing, 8
    leads to accounts, converting, 39
    multiple entities, searching
        across, 10
    new accounts, creating, 2
    opportunity from account,
        creating, 44
    ownership, changing, 14

    printing account view, 9
    searching for, 10
    sharing access to, 11
    sub accounts, creating, 3
    territories, changing, 12
    viewing
        access list for account, 13
        hierarchy of accounts, 8
        lists, 6
        printing account view, 9
Accounts tab, 2
ACT! version 4-6, importing data
    from, 225
activities. *See also* **events**
    completing, 91–92
    customizing settings for, 234
    details, viewing, 89
    home page, viewing activities on,
        88
addresses, mass updating of, 228
Advanced Search function
    for accounts, 10
    for opportunities, 53
advertising campaigns, 128

Working with Accounts

Create a new account
❶ Choose the Account option from the New drop-down on the left.

Edit an existing account
❶ Use the search tool on the left to find your account.
❷ Click the name of the account to edit it.

Delete an account
❶ Click an account to edit it.
❷ Click the Delete button.

Print an account list
❶ Click the Printable View link in the upper right.

Find an account
❶ Use the search area on the left column.

Working with Contacts

Create a new contact
❶ Go to the Contacts tab.
❷ Click the New button.

Delete a contact
❶ Go to a contact record.
❷ Click the Delete button.

View contact hierarchy
❶ Go to a contact record.
❷ Click the Delete button.

Duplicate a Contact
❶ Go to a contact record.
❷ Click View Org Chart link next to the Reports To field.

Send a Stay-in-Touch Request
❶ Go to a contact.
❷ Click the Request Update button.

Searching for a contact
❶ On the left column, locate the search area.
❷ Choose contacts from the drop-down and enter a search term in the field.

Working with Leads

Enter a new lead
❶ Choose the Lead option from the Create New drop-down on the left.

View available leads
❶ Go to the Leads tab.
❷ Choose a lead list view from the drop-down.

Convert a lead to an account
❶ Go to a lead record.
❷ Click the Convert button.

Managing Opportunities

Create a new opportunity
❶ Go to the Opportunities tab.
❷ Click the New button.

Add products to an opportunity
❶ When adding an opportunity, click the Add Product button in the Products area.

Create an opportunity from a contact
❶ In the Contacts tab, go to a contact record.
❷ Click the Create New drop-down on the left and choose Opportunity.

List Views

View a list of records
❶ Go to the tab that houses the type of information you'd like to see.
❷ Click the View drop-down and choose a list view.

Create a new list view
❶ Go to a tab that has list views.
❷ Click the Create New View link.

Edit an existing list view
❶ From the View drop-down, choose a list view.
❷ Click the Edit link to edit the list view definition.

Scheduling Activities

Install Connect for Outlook for Outlook calendar integration
❶ Click Setup | Desktop Integration | Connect for Outlook.

View your calendar
❶ Click the Home tab.
❷ Scroll down to the Calendar area.

Create an Event
❶ Go to the Calendar section of the Home page.
❷ Click the New Event button.

Create a Task
❶ Choose the Task option from the Create New drop-down on the left.

Sending E-mail

Send an e-mail to a contact
❶ Go to a contact record and scroll down to the Activity History related list.
❷ Click the Send An Email button.

Send a template-based e-mail
❶ Follow the steps above.
❷ When you are creating the message, click the Select Template button.

Create an Event
❶ Go to the Calendar section of the Home page.
❷ Click the New Event button.

Attach files to an e-mail
❶ When creating the message, click the Attach to Email button.

AppExchange

Access the AppExchange
❶ Click the AppExchange logo in the far upper right corner of Salesforce.

Writing Letters

Install Word integration
❶ Click Setup | Personal Setup | Desktop Integration | Connect for Microsoft Office.

Create a word template for mail merge
❶ Open Microsoft Word.
❷ Login to Salesforce by clicking on the Salesforce.com pull-down.

Upload a Word template to Salesforce.
❶ Click Setup | Administration Setup | Communication Templates | Mail Merge Templates.

Sending a letter to a contact
❶ Go to a contact record and scroll down to the Activity History section.
❷ Click the Mail Merge button.

Working Offline

Install Offline Edition
❶ Click Setup | Desktop Integration | Force.com Connect Offline.

Launch Offline Edition
❶ Click Start | Programs | Salesforce.com | Offline Edition.
❷ Enter your username and password. (When entering your password, make sure you add the full security token to the end of your password.)

Reset the Security Token

Reset your security token
❶ Click Setup | My Personal Information | Reset Security Token.
❷ Check your e-mail for the new security token.

Reports & Dashboards

Run a report
❶ From the Reports tab, click the name of the report you'd like to run.

Import Salesforce reports in Excel*
❶ In Excel, click the Salesforce button and login.
❷ Click the Salesforce button and choose the Import a Report option.
* Connect for Office required.

Customize a report
❶ Run a report.
❷ Click the Customize button.

View a dashboard
❶ Go to the Dashboard tab.
❷ Click the Go to Dashboard List link and select the dashboard to display.

Administering Campaigns

Create a new campaign
❶ Go to the Campaign tab and click the New button.

Add contacts to a campaign
❶ From the Campaign tab, click the name of a campaign.
❷ Click the Manage Members button.

Update a campaign
❶ Click the Manage Members button.
❷ Click the Update Status link.

Working with PDAs

Set up Salesforce Mobile
❶ Ask your Salesforce administrator to send you the Salesforce Mobile e-mail.
❷ Click the link in the-mail to install and configure Salesforce Mobile on your PDA.

Maximizing Your Sales with
Salesforce.com

| Home | Campaigns | Leads | Accounts | Contacts | Opportunities | Forecasts | Contracts | Cases | Solutions | Products | Reports | Documents | Dashboards |

Salesforce Logo. The logo in the upper left corner shows the current version of Salesforce. New versions are delivered automatically.

Setup. Go here to configure preferences, create templates, and set defaults for yourself or others.

Help. If you can't figure out the answer in this book, check out the online help. Interactive training lessons are also available in the help section.

The AppExchange. The AppExchange is a directory of add-on products that integrate directly with Salesforce.

Search. Use this quick search area to find specific contacts, accounts, leads, opportunities, cases, campaigns, contracts, tasks, and more.

Create New. Use this drop-down to create a new record of any type.

Recent Items. Instantly see a list of recently viewed items. This list will show accounts, contacts, leads, opportunities, and more.

Recycle Bin. See a list of everything you've deleted in the last 30 days.

Tabs. Tabs define the main organizational structure in Salesforce. Looking for everyone at XYZ Company? Go to the Accounts tab. Need to check if there are any new leads to work on? Go to the Leads tab.

Information. Depending on the tab you're in, you'll see different information in the main part of the Salesforce interface. You might see a list of contacts, details of a specific opportunity, or setup options.

Quick Create. Quickly create a new record. If you're in the Accounts tab, this area will create a new account. If you're in the Contacts tab, it will create a new contact.

Reports. Quickly run reports in your current tab. If you're in the Accounts tab, you'll see account reports. If you're in the Opportunities tab, you'll see opportunity reports.

Tools. Many of the tabs have a tools area that lets you perform administrative tasks -- like import -- for the data contained in the tab.

Finding Records

On the left column on most Salesforce pages, you'll see a search drop-down and field. Choose a record type from the drop-down, and enter a search term in the field.

Quick Tips FOR Creating & Deleting Records

CREATING NEW RECORDS

On most screens, you will see a Create New drop-down on the left. Use this drop-down to create any new record.

Anytime you see a New button, you can create a new record.

USING THE QUICK CREATE FEATURE

With a single click, you can create a new record using the Quick Create feature. You'll find it on the left side of many Salesforce pages.

UNDELETING RECORDS

On the left, click the Recycle Bin to bring up a list of everything you've deleted in the last 30 days.

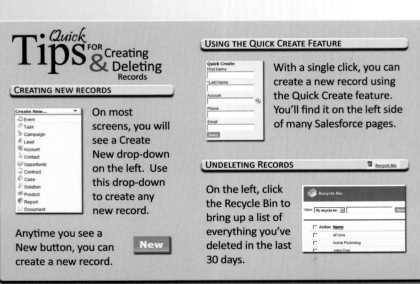

Useful Salesforce Web Sites:

http://trust.salesforce.com
Realtime server statistics and virus alerts:

http://ideas.salesforce.com
Submit feature requests and share ideas.

http://blog.sforce.com
Interact with Salesforce staff and users.

CENGAGE Learning

Maximizing Your Sales With Salesforce.com
Kachinske • Roach • Gilliland • Kachinske